AMSTERDAM'S GLORY

AMSTERDAM'S GLORY

The Old Masters of the City of Amsterdam

Norbert Middelkoop
Tom van der Molen

THOTH PUBLISHERS BUSSUM
AMSTERDAM HISTORICAL MUSEUM

COLOPHON

This publication accompanies *Old Masters of Amsterdam*, an exhibition at the Amsterdam
Historical Museum from 6 March to 9 August 2009

COVER ILLUSTRATION
Jan ten Compe, *Mint Tower viewed from Singel Canal*, 1751
Panel, 56 × 75.5 cm, Amsterdam Historical Museum

ILLUSTRATION P. 2-3
Gerrit Berckheyde, *Dam Square with the New Town Hall* (detail), c. 1665-70
Canvas, 75.5 × 91.5 cm, Amsterdam Historical Museum
ILLUSTRATION P. 6
Arent Arentsz called Cabel, *Winter Scene on the IJ at Amsterdam* (detail), c. 1621-23
Panel, 52.5 × 99 cm, Amsterdam Historical Museum
ILLUSTRATION P. 20-21
The Blockhouses in the Amstel River in Winter (detail), c. 1651-54
Canvas, 47.5 × 56 cm, Amsterdam Historical Museum

© 2009 The authors and THOTH Publishers, Nieuwe 's-Gravelandseweg 3, 1405 HH Bussum
WWW.THOTH.NL
WWW.AHM.NL

TRANSLATION
Sammy Herman, Jerusalem
GRAPHIC DESIGN
Ronald Boiten and Irene Mesu, Amersfoort
PRINTING
Drukkerij Mart. Spruijt bv, Amsterdam
BINDING
Boekbinderij Van Waarden, Zaandam

ISBN 978 90 6868 497 1

CONTENTS

FOREWORD

When the Amsterdam Historical Museum opened on Kalverstraat in 1975, it was a revelation. Under the enthusiastic leadership of director Simon Levie and curator Bob Haak, a magnificently restored edifice, the historic complex of the former Civic Orphanage, was transformed into an extensive, contemporary museum in which art, archaeological and historical objects, memorabilia and innovative multimedia displays were brought together to present the broad spectrum of the city's history to the general public. To catch the visitor's eye, the architects developed the Civic Guard Gallery: an enclosed section of street in which, when the museum was open, passers-by and people walking through town could admire a selection of civic guard portraits at no cost. For the display on the walls of this spectacular site and for the displays in the museum itself, Levie and Haak set their sights on part of the city of Amsterdam's art collection that had been given on loan to the Rijksmuseum in 1885. The return of these exhibits involved tough negotiations. At the Rijksmuseum it was feared that these works of art would be downgraded if they were exhibited as mere historical documents.

The museum's presentation has remained much the same since it opened in 1975. The paintings in the permanent presentation form a key element in the chronological story of the city down the centuries. Major works by Berckheyde, Bol, Jacob Cornelisz, Flinck, Van der Helst, Van der Heyden, Hondecoeter and Mierevelt have been augmented over the years with works by De Hooch, Rembrandt and Ruisdael. A look through the pages of *Amsterdam's Glory* gives an excellent idea of the tremendous quality of the paintings collection.

While the aesthetic pleasure provided by this display of art is undoubted, ours would not be the Amsterdam Historical Museum if we did not present the history at the same time. In fact the descriptions of the highlights selected for this publication focus above all on their historical background: first and foremost, their provenance. A perusal of the texts reveals to the reader something of the mystery why so much incredible art was produced in Holland's Golden Age: there was a huge demand for art, and the greatest patrons were the city's countless institutions and organisations. The burgomasters, the admiralty, the Dutch East India Company, the civic guard, the numerous charities and the Surgeons' Guild; they immortalised their ambitions, status and achievements in paintings that hung on the walls of the places in which they assembled. As society modernised, particularly in the nineteenth century, many of these bodies were disbanded. That was when their paintings came into the possession of the city. *Amsterdam's Glory* attempts to trace the original provenance and significance of these paintings.

Interestingly, many of the buildings in which the paintings were originally displayed still exist. A short walk along Gelderse Kade and Kloveniersburgwal, for example, already takes in six of these locations: Schreierstoren, Weigh House, Trippenhuis, Madhouse, Oudemanhuispoort and Doelen Hotel. Even the Amsterdam Historical Museum itself, once the Civic Orphanage, is the original home of some of the finest group portraits, as the presentation in the governors' boardroom shows. *Amsterdam's Glory* is about more than just the paintings, it is about the city's many historical monuments as well.

It only remains to express a few words of thanks. In the first place, full praise to the curator and author Norbert Middelkoop for his efforts in realising this project, which began with the publication of the large museum catalogue *De oude meesters van de stad Amsterdam. Schilderijen tot 1800* (published in 2008, also by THOTH). Tom van der Molen was his assistant in that project and wrote the descriptions in *Amsterdam's Glory* to make the masterpieces accessible for a wider public. Finally, the staff of the collections department spared no effort to ensure that the works were properly restored and reproduced for the publication and the greater glory of the Amsterdam Historical Museum!

Paul Spies, Director

AMSTERDAM COLLECTING OLD MASTERS

Norbert Middelkoop

'A large, handsome room that looks out onto the large courtyard of the girl's house. The chimney and walls are decorated with three paintings of governors and two of governesses.' This description, written in 1760 by Jan Wagenaar, historian of Amsterdam, is of the Governors' Room of the Civic Orphanage on Kalverstraat. Centuries have passed, and Amsterdam has changed in many ways. The historic complex of the Civic Orphanage, for example, is now home to the Amsterdam Historical Museum. Yet the former Governors' Room still exudes that same atmosphere which Wagenaar encountered (fig. 1). The group portraits he mentions have been preserved and can be seen in the very building for which they were intended. One is a portrait of governesses, painted by Adriaen Backer in 1683 (fig. 2). Four fashionably attired ladies are seated at the boardroom table, while the matron on the right brings in two orphans in threadbare clothes. The maid is entering on the left, carrying the orphanage's red and black uniforms. It is an obvious

1 The Governors' Room at the former Civic Orphanage (now Amsterdam Historical Museum) Photo AHM

2 Adriaen Backer (1635/36-1684), *The Governesses of the Civic Orphanage*, 1683. Canvas, 193 × 282 cm. Amsterdam Historical Museum, on loan from Spirit

message. Besides being good administrators, these governesses are also good people, and the children are in good hands.

That the orphanage's paintings have remained in their original location all these years is remarkable. The collection of paintings accumulated by the city of Amsterdam has grown over a long period of time, prompted originally by the need to look after works of art that had become homeless, and motivated later by the desire to create a museum collection. The collection's history is inextricably bound with the manner of its display: from decoration of civic guard buildings and governors' boardrooms to museum object at the Amsterdam Historical Museum and Rijksmuseum. The city currently owns around 2,500 paintings, of which a thousand date from before 1800: so-called Old Masters. The core of this part of the collection is an incomparable series of group portraits, divided roughly into portraits of civic guards and portraits of governors. Originally, the governors' portraits adorned the official rooms of the city's care and correctional institutions, such as the Leper House, the Work House and the Civic Orphanage. Dozens of civic guard portraits were displayed in the three *doelens* belonging to the Longbow, Crossbow and Harquebusier civic guard. In and around the rooms where these paintings were displayed, men would practise their weapons, eat and drink. On the walls were the sixteenth- and seventeenth-century portraits of the men of various squads and companies, commanded by a captain and a lieutenant, and invariably accompanied by an ensign bearing the colours.

A popular attraction was the guild-room of the Surgeons' Guild. This was at the Weigh House on Nieuwmarkt square where a famous collection of anatomy lessons could be seen. Today's museum visitor may find it hard to believe that so many wonderful works of art were painted in a single city in the space of so few decades. Yet Amsterdam's economic success in that Golden Age produced a deluge of commissions for

paintings, from middle-class burghers as well as wealthy patricians. The inevitable competition among artists laid the foundation for the high quality of their work.

Paintings on the Move

In 1683, civic guard portraits began to be brought over from the civic guard buildings to the Town Hall on Dam Square, currently the Royal Palace. The removal of these paintings reflects the stagnation of Amsterdam's economy at this time. There were no funds for a new programme of extensive decoration for the top floor of the town hall. Yet a more appropriate furnishing for the courts martial on the third floor could hardly have been imagined than these group portraits of the city's illustrious civic guard companies. After all, this was where the ultimate authority over the civic guard rested. Of the paintings brought to the town hall, Rembrandt's *Night Watch* (fig. 3) is by far the most famous. When it was transferred in 1715, part of the canvas was cut away, to match the length of the wall. Later in the same century, Rembrandt's *Syndics* (fig. 4) also came to the Town Hall, from the Cloth Hall.

3 Rembrandt (1606-1669), *The Night Watch*, 1642. Canvas, 359 × 438 cm. Rijksmuseum, on loan from the city of Amsterdam

4 Rembrandt,
The Syndics, 1662.
Canvas, 191.5 × 279 cm.
Rijksmuseum, on
loan from the city of
Amsterdam

In April 1806, the city opened a modest presentation of curiosities on the third floor of the Town Hall to the public. Among the items on show were the *Adoration* fragment by Pieter Aertsen, the remains of a lost altarpiece that had probably been in the city's possession since 1578 (see p. 29). So too the famous *Bird's-Eye View* by Cornelis Anthonisz of 1538 (see p. 26-27). The exhibition did not last long. Searching for a suitable residence, King Louis Bonaparte eventually selected the Town Hall. Renamed the Royal Palace, the building was emptied in March 1808, with the exception of the permanently fixed paintings. Louis Bonaparte set aside the same rooms that had housed the city's collection for a Royal Museum. Here the king ordered seven paintings from the municipal collection to be shown, among them Govert Flinck's *Civic Guard Banquet* (p. 51), Rembrandt's *Night Watch* and *Syndics*, as well as Van de Velde's *Gouden Leeuw* from Schreierstoren (p. 91).

When the French occupation ended in 1813, the new Dutch king, Willem I, moved the Royal Museum to the Trippenhuis on Kloveniersburgwal. The seven paintings that had been lent by the city for the presentation at the palace were also moved to the new Rijks Museum, which opened in 1817 (fig. 5). All the other paintings along with

5 Isaac Ouwater (1748-1793), *The Trippenhuis on Kloveniersburgwal*, 1783 (?). Canvas, 48 × 62 cm. **Amsterdam Historical Museum**

6 Johan M. A. Rieke (1851-1899),
*The Exhibition of Curiosities at
the Prinsenhof, c.*1880-85.
Amsterdam City Archive

7 J.B. Bickhoff, *The Burgomaster and Aldermen's
Room at the Prinsenhof.* Photo *c.* 1917.
Amsterdam City Archive

the city's collection of curiosities were transferred to a location not far from there: in the public rooms, offices and corridors of the new town hall that had recently opened at the Prinsenhof on Oudezijds Voorburgwal. The principal works of art and historical exhibits were shown in presentations on the building's top floor (fig. 6). New objects were regularly added to the collection. For example when the Old Men and Women's Almshouse closed in 1842, six large paintings were brought to the Prinsenhof. The closure of the Leper House in 1859 led to a new influx, including some works that were immediately given a prominent place. Ferdinand Bol's earliest group portrait of governors was actually displayed in the burgomaster and aldermen's room (fig. 7 and p. 58).

In the spring of 1854, the city found itself with a problem: what do with the remarkable gift bequeathed to Amsterdam by Adriaan van der Hoop. Over the course of twenty years, this hugely wealthy banker had built up a major collection of paintings, mainly by seventeenth-century Dutch and Flemish masters. He had been interested in every genre, and had attempted to acquire at least one work by each of the principal masters. In addition, the banker had also encouraged contemporary artists by buying their work. The focus of the collection was small cabinet pictures: landscapes, marines and figures, including portraits, city views and still lifes. One exception was the large *Allegory of the Expansion of Amsterdam* by Berchem (see p. 69), that had adorned Van der Hoop's stairwell. Following an appeal among wealthy private donors to pay the inheritance tax, the city was

8 Rembrandt, *The Jewish Bride*. Canvas, 121.5 × 166.5 cm. Rijksmuseum, on loan from the city of Amsterdam

9 Johannes Vermeer (1632-1675), *Woman Reading a Letter*. Canvas, 46.5 × 39 cm. Rijksmuseum, on loan from the city of Amsterdam

able to accept the bequest and take over the 224 paintings. Soon after, the Van der Hoop Museum opened in the building of the Royal Academy of Fine Arts, at the former Old Men and Women's Almshouse. Today, most of the Van der Hoop collection is at the Rijksmuseum, on loan from the city. Its star attractions are Rembrandt's *Jewish Bride* and Vermeer's *Woman Reading a Letter* (fig. 8 and 9).

The city's art collection received another significant injection in 1864, this time with the acquisition of the Surgeons' Guild collection of paintings. The former owners, the penurious surgeons' widows fund, had already cashed in their two anatomy lessons by Rembrandt. His *Anatomy Lesson of Dr Nicolaes Tulp* had been put up for auction in 1828, and snapped up before the sale by Willem I for the Royal Cabinet of Paintings in The Hague, today's Mauritshuis. Thirteen years later, the *Anatomy Lesson of Dr Jan Deyman* (p. 60) had been purchased by a London dealer. A committee of Amsterdam's art enthusiasts, artists and doctors succeeded in buying the remaining paintings for 6,000 guilders, aided by donations from other connoisseurs. The works were moved to rooms at Athenaeum Illustre (the forerunner of Amsterdam University), then located in the former headquarters of the Longbowmen on Singel canal.

Major Exhibitions

In the course of the nineteenth century, the cry for a permanent exhibition space for the city's art collection grew louder. A significant boost came with a series of shows of paintings held in Amsterdam in 1845, 1867 and 1872, to which the city lent generously (fig. 10). The organisers were motivated by a wish to encourage more people to become aware of art and to inspire young artists. At first, commentators praised these exhibitions; later they were more critical, noting how many portraits of civic guards and governors had been extracted for public display 'from dark town halls and institutions'. The realisation, no less in government circles, that these art treasures deserved more, breathed new life into the dormant plans for a new Rijksmuseum. This would provide a home for the Trippenhuis collection, as well as the 'many masterpieces that are now found in the town hall and other civic institutions'.

The largest of all these exhibitions was the Historical Exhibition of 1876, organised to mark Amsterdam's six-hundredth anniversary. The Van der Hoop Museum

10 The grand salon at *Arti en Amicitiae* during the exhibition of rare and important old master paintings, 1872, engraving from Henry Havard, *Amsterdam et Venise* (Paris 1876)

was emptied for the presentation and part of the collection removed. The show provided a chronological survey of the city's history, displaying both paintings and art objects, 4,371 in all. Once again, the city was the principal lender. Encouraged by the exhibition's success, the Royal Antiquarian Society succeeded in establishing a museum as a small-scale continuation of the exhibition: the *Amsterdamsch Museum* (fig. 11). Despite the municipality's original interest, this precursor of today's Amsterdam Historical Museum did not survive long. Four months later, the city informed the society that the venue would be needed for the projected Exhibition of Living Masters. It seems that the plans for the new Rijksmuseum, to which the municipality was now firmly committed, had brought an untimely end to the *Amsterdamsch Museum*.

As criticism of the display and storage of the city's paintings mounted, exacerbated by the debacle of the *Amsterdamsch Museum*, on 1 January 1878 the municipality set up a committee to advise and supervise the city of Amsterdam's paintings. Its purpose was to recommend a solution to the municipality for the location and preservation of its paintings, against the many bureaucratic and financial constraints. As more ancient institutions closed, the number of paintings increased: from 138 in 1864, to 179 by 1878. Most of these were at the town hall at the Prinsenhof, 'in rooms in which the atmosphere is continually polluted by the perspiration and exhalation of the many people that constantly accumulate in these rooms, while paintings hang in halls and corridors where the public wanders around without any supervision.' The committee also looked into the sorry state of the Van der Hoop Museum. Its 224 paintings had already been earmarked *en bloc* to be lent to the proposed new Rijksmuseum. One of the committee's first achievements was to ensure that some large paintings were removed from the town hall to the new State Academy of Fine Arts on Stadhouderskade. These ample walls also provided space for Athenaeum's collection of paintings from the Surgeons' Guild. In 1882, a member of the committee, Jan Six VII, discovered the fragment of Rembrandt's *Anatomy Lesson of Dr Jan Deyman* in storage at London's South Kensington Museum, forty years after it had left Amsterdam. A new appeal was launched and private donors raised 1,400 guilders to buy the painting back for the city: the centrepiece of the anatomy lessons collection.

New Museums

As agreed, in 1885 the city of Amsterdam entrusted most of its art treasures to the new Rijksmuseum (fig. 12). This included the seven large Trippenhuis canvases, the entire Van der Hoop Museum inventory and most of the items at the State Academy of Fine Arts, as well as 24 paintings from the Poor House and a collection of 44 important family portraits left by Jeanne Cathérine Bicker, of that prominent Amsterdam family. Of the items selected for removal from the Prinsenhof, the Rijksmuseum received most of what it wanted. There remained a number of paintings in the burgomaster and aldermen's room, the assembly room and other official rooms. In the years following the opening, new items were regularly added to the loan agreement. After the closure of Felix Meritis in 1888, for example, the museum received four group portraits of members of the society by Adriaan de Lelie, on loan from the city (see p. 106-107). As a matter of course, the municipality also sent works left by private

11 Pieter Oosterhuis (1816-1885),
The Amsterdamsch Museum. Photo 1877

individuals to the city to the Rijksmuseum, the finest of these being Jan van der Heyden's *Dam Square* (p. 73), which J. F. van Lennep had stipulated shortly before his death in 1892 should come to hang in the Rijksmuseum.

Two major legacies went to two entirely different destinations. The estate left by the wealthy widow Sophia Adriana Lopez Suasso-de Bruijn in 1890 formed the foundation for the construction of today's Stedelijk Museum on Van Baerlestraat, a few hundred metres from the Rijksmuseum. Her collection, an eclectic mix of dolls, jewellery, books, applied art and paintings would be presented in period rooms on the ground floor. Jacob de Wit's ceiling painting was also transferred to the building (fig. 13), a gift from Pieter de Clercq and Pieter van Eeghen. A completely separate museum was created for the Willet-Holthuysen collection. Before her death in 1895, Louise Willet-Holthuysen stipulated that her enormous collection of applied art, books, prints, photos and paintings which she was leaving to the city, should remain in its entirety in the house in which she and her husband had lived. This museum on Herengracht, named after them, still exists.

In response to increasing criticism regarding the presentation and functioning of the Rijksmuseum, the government appointed a commission in 1918 to advise on the reorganisation of the country's national museums. In its final report, the commission proposed that the collections be divided into three groups: objects of exceptional artistic merit, those of art-historical significance and those of historical interest. Amsterdam occupied a unique position, since 'Due to the tremendous flowering of the arts within its confines, this city is richer than any other in works of art of local significance. It has a huge series of paintings extending from the modest beginnings of the sixteenth century to the heights of Rembrandt's *Night Watch* and *Syndics* and then through the ebb of the eighteenth to the early nineteenth century with one or two works of importance.' Art works of the first order in the city's collection should, according to the report, be displayed in a general art museum to form part of the Rijksmuseum. The Van der Hoop Museum should be split into 'old and so-called semi-modern art, into masterpieces and works of lesser quality'. Paintings of art-historical importance should be shown in a historical

12 Johannes Hilverdink (1813-1902), *The Rijksmuseum*, 1885. Canvas, 66 × 106 cm. Amsterdam Historical Museum

13 Jacob de Wit (1695-1754), *Sunrise Dispels the Night*, 1744. Canvas, 370 × 520 cm. Museum Willet Holthuysen

museum within the Rijksmuseum. The remaining paintings 'of no significant artistic value, no art-historical importance and without historical interest' could then be allocated to a local Amsterdam historical museum. The weigh house on Nieuwmarkt square would in the commission's opinion form an excellent venue for a 'collection of Amsterdam antiquities and curiosities of a folkloristic nature'. Moreover, 'the town hall, Stedelijk museum and municipal archive still had many portraits and city views that were nowhere more perfectly suited'.

Amsterdam Historical Museum at the Weigh House

The recommendations of the government commission provided a guideline for the establishment of the proposed historical museum. This gained added momentum in 1925 with the Historical Exhibition marking the 65oth anniversary of Amsterdam at the Stedelijk Museum and Rijksmuseum. For the show, the seventeenth-century highlights at the Rijksmuseum were joined by works lent from the town hall in the Prinsenhof, some of which remained at the museum after the exhibition. As compensation, the Rijksmuseum earmarked dozens of paintings for the new museum at the weigh house, including 36 that had originally been lent by the city. Among these were seven group portraits from the Surgeons' Guild (though not Rembrandt's *Deyman* fragment) which now returned to the building for which they had been intended – the guild had been based at the Weigh House. On 1 November 1926, the long-awaited Amsterdam Historical Museum opened. Its main attraction was not a painting, but the sculpture group of David and Goliath, also returned by the Rijksmuseum (fig. 14).

In those early years the museum had no acquisitions policy as such. Amsterdam's art dealers responded adroitly to the young museum's needs by placing a regular supply of affordable city views in their shop windows. These were relatively under-represented in the collection and the museum was apparently attempting to correct the imbalance. With its numerous purchases, the museum had constantly to raise money to pay off debts, interrupted occasionally by opportunities to acquire paintings on some other basis. At a hundred pounds Sterling (around 730 guilders), Ten Compe's *Mint* (p. 102) seemed beyond reach in 1936, until it emerged that a member of the museum committee had bought the panel to donate it to the museum.

It was also clear that another way of adding to the collection would be to revise the loan arrangement with the Rijksmuseum. To enhance the chronological overview of Amsterdam's history, in 1934 the museum drew up a list of works which, as a municipal institution, it now sought back from the national institution on Museumplein. After all, many of the group portraits on loan from the city were being held in storage there. These requests met with vehement resistance from

Museumplein, where the young municipal museum's ambitions were viewed with suspicion. The history of Amsterdam in its national context was the Rijksmuseum's province; local urban history was for the Weigh House, they reasoned. Apart from two surgeon paintings and one Felix Meritis painting by De Lelie, the requested works remained where they were, although three other paintings were given on loan by the state.

During the Second World War, when the Netherlands was occupied (1940-1945), the museum managed to acquire a few paintings from the pre-1800 period, including a portrait of Gerrit Jacobsz Witsen by Mierevelt (fig. 15), which was purchased in January 1944 for 19,000 guilders. An interesting aspect is the hope expressed at the time by the museum's director that 'the city will probably be able to exchange this portrait after the war for a portrait of the famous burgomaster Corn. Pietersz. Hooft by Van der Voort, which would be a far more significant acquisition for the Amsterdam Historical Museum from a historical perspective' (see p. 36). Today, both burgomasters are on show at the museum. Shortly

14 **The Amsterdam Historical Museum at the Weigh House, November 1926. Amsterdam City Archive**

15 Michiel van Mierevelt, *Gerrit Jacobsz Witsen, c.* 1620-26.
Panel, 117 × 90 cm.
Amsterdam Historical Museum

after the war the museum made another important acquisition: the *Surgeon's Workplace* by Egbert van Heemskerck, purchased from the Oranje Appel Orphanage (see p. 77). The price of 3,000 guilders was paid in installments over three years.

In 1954, the Willet Holthuysen Museum acquired the Backer foundation collection on long-term loan. The agreement included dozens of portraits of members of this family of Amsterdam patricians and was later extended to include even more. An ample selection of these remarkable works can be seen on the walls of the museum on Herengracht to this day.

A major setback was the failure to ensure that the city of Amsterdam secured the collection built up by Willem Dreesmann, who died in that same year. Attempts to acquire his valuable accumulation of 'Amstelodamensia' and to incorporate it into the Amsterdam Historical Museum came to nothing. Even so, with support from the city and donations from private benefactors the museum was nevertheless able to acquire many items when the collection went up for sale in 1960.

The Dreesmann auction brought the Amsterdam Historical Museum's plan to move into the Civic Orphanage complex on Kalverstraat to a head. In 1962, the city of Amsterdam purchased the buildings, taking over the orphanage's art collection on long-term loan. Director Simon Levie and assistant director Bob Haak, curator of paintings, were the driving force behind the substantial reconstruction and refurbishing of the interior. In addition to a series of crucial purchases, they also negotiated with the directors of the Rijksmuseum for a revision of the loan agreement of 1885. They wished to display a large number of paintings still on loan from the city to the Rijksmuseum in the new Amsterdam Historical Museum. Although the talks were sometimes fraught – Rijksmuseum director Arthur van Schendel feared that these masterpieces would be degraded to the status of historical documents – by the summer of 1971 agreement had been reached in principle. Unfortunately, the main stumbling block, that one of the four Rembrandt's owned by the city be made available, was not resolved. In the end, 156 paintings and four pastels from the city's collection were transferred to the Amsterdam Historical Museum, along with 70 paintings from the Rijksmuseum itself.

The New Amsterdam Historical Museum
When the Amsterdam Historical Museum opened at its new home on 27 October 1975, the presentation focused on the seventeenth century, the period represented by the most and the largest paintings in the collection. A spectacular, freely accessible Civic Guard Gallery provided ample space for an excellent selection of group portraits (fig. 16). After Levie moved to the Rijksmuseum, Haak continued his predecessor's policy as the new director. His significant acquisitions of old masters included Cabel's *Winter Scene on the IJ*, Ruisdael's *Kostverloren Manor* and Beerstraaten's *Burning of the Old Town Hall* (p. 37, 82 and 55).

A significant achievement came later, thanks to one of Haak's successors at the Amsterdam Historical Museum, Pauline Kruseman, and Henk van Os, Levie's successor at the Rijksmuseum, namely the resolution of the Rembrandt question: the stalemate resulting from the desire to display one of the city's four Rembrandts at the Amsterdam Historical Museum. Following a major Rembrandt exhibition that showed in Amsterdam, London and Berlin, the restored fragment of the *Anatomy Lesson of Dr Jan Deyman* (p. 60) was transferred to the museum in 1994 and welcomed in a special presentation. It fitted perfectly with the existing display of paintings from the Surgeons' Guild, with which it still hangs. Several major purchases were also made under Kruseman, including the only identified family group portrait by Pieter de Hooch and a magnificent *View of Amsterdam* by Jacob van Ruisdael (p. 78 and 83).

Most of the great names of Dutch art are represented in the city's collection, as painters of the many group portraits of civic guard companies and governors, allegories and city views. It was private initiative that first encouraged the municipal authority to realise the importance of taking responsibility for its cultural heritage. Without the exertions of art enthusiasts in the nineteenth and early twentieth century, today's magnificent displays of the city's art treasures at the Rijksmuseum and the Amsterdam Historical Museum would have looked quite different. Thanks to their concern and effort, the city managed to retain many paintings. In the museum age, directors and curators have been able to add many major works to the old master collection. Together they form the rich heritage of Amsterdam.

This text is an adapted and translated summary of an earlier essay by the author in *De Oude Meesters van de stad Amsterdam. Schilderijen tot 1800* (Amsterdam/Bussum 2008).

16 The Civic Guard gallery of the Amsterdam Historical Museum, early 1990s.
Photo AHM

Masterpieces

OF THE AMSTERDAM
HISTORICAL MUSEUM

These two fragments of an altarpiece from Agnietenkapel (St Agnes's chapel) in Amsterdam depict the patrons who donated the work. The figures would originally have appeared kneeling either side of a religious scene. What that may have been is no longer known, but what appears to be part of a cloak below right on the left panel may have belonged to Mary Magdalen, in which case it was probably a Crucifixion, flanked by the couple's patron saints.

The man furthest forward on the left panel is Corsgen Elbertsen. His wife, Geerte Hendricksdr. van der Schelling is the furthest left on the right segment. In front of her is their daughter Margriet, who entered St Agnes convent and served as abbess from 1531 to 1556. Her sister Baerte, behind her, was also a nun at the convent. The third daughter, Engeltje, married Heymen Jacobsz van der Ouder-Amstel. The other women and girls are daughters and granddaughters of Corsgen and Geerte who have not been identified.

The men standing behind Corsgen on the left panel are his sons, Dirck and Albert, and perhaps also his son-in-law Heymen.

These two panels were acquired by a curious chance. Until 1923, the two panels were at Berlin's Kaiser Friedrich Museum. That was when they were recognised and an exchange was arranged for a group portrait of governors by Werner van den Valckert.

PORTRAITS OF THE DONORS, THE CORSGEN ELBERTSEN-VAN DER SCHELLING FAMILY
c. 1500-18

Jacob Cornelisz (War) van Oostsanen
(Oostzaan 1472/77–in or before 1533 Amsterdam)

Panel, 90 × 57 cm (left panel), 89 × 73 cm (right panel)

One of the seminal events in the early history of Amsterdam was the miracle that took place in the city in 1345. On 15 March of that year, a dying man received the last rites. Later that night he vomited the sacramental wafer with his food, which the attending nurse cleared up and threw into the fire. But the wafer survived the flames unscathed. The next day, the nurse found it as she cleaned the smouldering ashes from the hearth and placed it in a box. She told the priest who had given the last rites. He took the wafer to the city's main church: the Oude Kerk. The following day the wafer was back in its box, in the old man's house. So the priest decided that the wafer should be brought to the church in a solemn procession.

The place where the miracle occurred on Kalverstraat soon began to attract pilgrims. In 1347 the wafer was placed in a monstrance on an altar, after the old man's house had been replaced by a chapel and a centre for pilgrimage.

Jacob Cornelisz van Oostsanen's work has not survived complete. He probably painted it as one long, horizontal banner showing seven scenes from the story. It was originally displayed at Nieuwezijds chapel, which was built on the site of the miracle. The remaining eight fragments show a number of scenes from the story of the miracle (see captions).

THE MIRACLE OF AMSTERDAM
C. 1515

Jacob Cornelisz (War) van Oostsanen
(Oostzaan 1472/77-in or before 1533 Amsterdam)

Tempera on canvas, 79,5 × 30 cm (left), 85,5 × 171,5 cm (middle), 113 × 41,5 cm (right)
On loan from the Protestant Community of Amsterdam

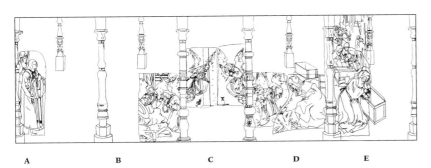

A   B   C   D   E

Proposed reconstruction of the banner
- A A priest performs the last rites;
- B Dying man vomits the sacramental wafer; Woman throws the vomit into the fire;
- C Wafer hovers above the fire; Angels wave incense;
- D Woman picks the wafer out of the fire; Wafer is placed in a box;
- E Woman kneels beside the box; Wafer is placed in a monstrance; Procession to the Oude Kerk; Placing the wafer in the chapel. Confirmation of the miracle in 1346.

Members of Amsterdam's militia began commissioning group portraits of their squads in 1529. This depiction of a squad painted by Cornelis Anthonisz in 1533 is the earliest known portrait of the men of the Crossbow guild.

The subjects are depicted eating a meal. There is bread on the table, with a plate of poultry and a herring. Maybe the rather sparse meal is where the painting gained its nickname in the eighteenth century: *The Braspenning Banquet*. A *braspenning* was a coin valued at slightly over five cent. Perhaps that is what the banquet is supposed to have cost.

The artist may have included himself in the painting, above left, just below his signature. He was indeed a member of the Crossbow guild. That they are crossbowmen is clear from the picture. Two of the men in the background are actually holding crossbows; each man is also wearing a miniature model of a crossbow as an insignia on the right sleeve of his uniform.

Above right is a stained-glass window depicting St George. He was the guild's patron saint.

Banquets were the highpoint of the year for the guards. They would eat and drink, and of course sing. One of the men is shown holding a sheet of music with the lyrics of a song entitled 'In mijne sinn heb ik vercooren een meysken' (In my heart I have chosen a girl).

THE BRASPENNING BANQUET
1533

Cornelis Anthonisz
(Amsterdam c. 1505-1553 Amsterdam)

Panel, 130 × 206.5 cm
Monogrammed and dated above left: *anno 1533*/CAT
(the A in the shape of a St Anthony bell)

One of the highlights in the civic guard year was the annual parrot-shooting contest. This target competition involved shooting a wooden parrot off a pole. The painting shows two winners, the so-called kings, with their prizes, a chain and royal sceptre.

The two winners are shown surrounded by the squad of harquebusiers in which they served. Harquebusier squads normally comprised thirteen men. In this painting there are fourteen, so there is one man extra. Perhaps one of the two winners was no longer part of the squad, posing with his one-time companions for the occasion.

It is unclear who painted this group portrait. The identity of the men in the painting is also unknown. No list of names has survived, as on other portraits of militia squads, where the various figures can be identified. We can say with reasonable certainty that the person pointed at by various members of the squad is probably the captain. He is clearly the senior figure in the portrait; it seems reasonable to assume that the men would focus their attention on the person highest in rank.

SQUAD OF HARQUEBUSIERS WITH TWO MILITIA KINGS
1534

Artist unknown

Panel, 125 × 225 cm
Dated on a board hanging from a tree,
top centre: *1534*

26

BIRD'S-EYE VIEW OF AMSTERDAM
1538

Cornelis Anthonisz
(Amsterdam c. 1505-1553 Amsterdam)

Panel, 116 × 159 cm
Monogrammed and dated left and right of the weathervane
below: *1538 CAT*

This painting, dating from 1538, is the earliest known map of Amsterdam. In fact it is a cross between a map and a view of the city. By looking at the city from an imaginary position high in the air, Cornelis Anthonisz was able to combine a detailed depiction of the buildings with a chart of the town walls, roads, river and waterways.

Clearly recognisable halfway along the Amstel, the river that divides the city in two, is Dam Square. To the right of the square stands the old Town Hall, with its central tower. Beside it is the Nieuwe Kerk. The Oude Kerk is the large building with the tower between Dam Square and the mouth of the Amstel. Left of this, Sint Anthonispoort (today's Weigh House) marks the city's eastern extremity. Further towards the harbor stands Schreierstoren, here still serving as a corner fort on the town wall.

Below right, the tip of the Volewijck peninsula is visible. This area, where today's ferry to north Amsterdam docks, was once the site of the city's public executions.

A payment to the artist is noted in the city's accounts of 1538: 'Cornelis Anthonisz, painter, for having drawn this city for my lord of Bossu to show to his Imperial Majesty. According to the commission and the receipt hereby paid the sum of 6 pounds.' It seems therefore that Jan van Hennin, Lord of Bossu, Charles V's representative in Amsterdam, intended to show the painting to the emperor. Although the painting probably never left the city, Charles V may have seen it when he visited Amsterdam in 1540.

During fire that engulfed the old Town Hall in 1652 (see p. 55) the panel was damaged. It was probably restored not long after. Jan Micker may have been the restorer, since he produced a loose copy of the work around this time (see p. 57).

The city of Amsterdam has four group portraits of civic guards that are so close in style that they are almost certainly the work of the same artist. Yet we have no name for this painter, which is why he has become known as the Master of the Antwerp Family Portrait, after a painting by the artist at the Royal Museum of Fine Arts in Antwerp.

These seventeen men served in F squad. Depicted in two rows, one above the other, the squad belonged to the Harquebusier guild. This is clear from four of the men holding a harquebus, a kind of musket. Some of the squad also have the harquebusier insignia on their sleeve: a bird's claw with a musket. A claw is also depicted on the dish held by the man top left. It refers to the guild's Dutch name: a harquebus is a *klover* and harquebusiers are *kloveniers*, or *clauweniers*, which relates to *klauw*, the word for claw.

A letter held by one of the figures in the portrait reveals the holder's identity. It states, 'Domino Cornelis / van Dellef / in / Amstredam'. Cornelis van Delft joined the harquebusiers in 1549.

SEVENTEEN MEN OF F SQUAD
1557
Master of the Antwerp Family Portrait

Panel 133 × 169.5 cm
Dated left on the wall: *1557*

This fragment of a much larger panel shows an ox looking straight at us. A shepherd is leaning over the animal, gazing at something happening to the left, out of our field of vision. This missing section would doubtless have shown the newborn infant Christ. Probably the white sheet on the left belongs to the crib. Behind the shepherd, identified by his crook, is another man, perhaps a second shepherd. The fragment was once part of a large altarpiece depicting the adoration of the shepherds. It was displayed at the Nieuwe Kerk and may have been broken up when the churches were ransacked in 1578. That was when the Catholic hegemony in Amsterdam ended and Protestants took over both church property and government: the Alteration. The fragment also survived the fire at the old town hall in 1652 (see p. 55).

Many writers who have discussed this work over the centuries, attributed it erroneously to Rubens. It was not until 1885 that it was definitely identified as being by Aertsen. He worked for many years in Antwerp, like Rubens fifty years later.

ADORATION OF THE SHEPHERDS (FRAGMENT)
c. 1559

Pieter Aertsen
(Amsterdam? 1507-1575 Amsterdam)

Panel, 89,8 × 59,2 cm

THE RETURN TO AMSTERDAM OF THE SECOND EXHIBITION TO THE EAST INDIES

1599

Hendrick Cornelisz Vroom
(Haarlem 1566-1640 Haarlem)

Canvas, 110 × 220 cm
On loan from the Rijksmuseum, Amsterdam

An inscription on the frame gives a precise summary of the scene portrayed in this painting by Hendrick Vroom. 'The first of May in the year 1598 / Mauritius, Hollandt, Overijssel and Vrieslant; Four ships sailed out to obtain spices / from Bantam and also cultivated trade there; and returned richly laden to Amsterdam's harbour on the nineteenth of July, 1599'. In the distance lies the city of Amsterdam; the four large ships are approaching, welcomed by a flotilla of small boats and barges. Salutes are fired all around. The four vessels mentioned in the inscription had set sail the previous year under the command of Jacob van Neck (1564-1638). They had reached Asia as planned and had returned bringing full cargos of expensive products, particularly spices.

In the sixteenth century, Spain and Portugal had dominated Europe's trade with Asia. A group of merchants in Amsterdam, who realised that this would be a highly lucrative business, combined forces and set up a company to send an expedition to the Far East. Their first fleet returned in 1597, without much success; the costs of the venture were not covered by the

profits. Yet they refused to give up. In 1598, the company sent the fleet shown in this picture on a similar errand. The expedition, which sailed to Bantam on West Java, made a huge profit. Jacob van Neck took a third fleet to Asia in 1600. On that voyage he visited China as well.

Other companies along the same lines as this Amsterdam venture

were set up elsewhere in the Dutch provinces of Holland and Zeeland. They sailed excellent, well-armed ships and proved tough rivals for the Spanish and Portuguese. They competed with each other too.

That was not a productive sort of competition. In 1602, Johan van Oldebarnevelt (1547-1619) brought and end to it by establishing a

united company, the Dutch East India Company (Verenigde Oostindische Compagnie or VOC). Not long after, it was granted a monopoly on Dutch trade in Asia. Moreover, the VOC was authorised to conclude treaties in the Dutch Republic's name, to fight wars and to administer captured territories. In 1619, Jan Pieterszoon Coen (1587-1629) founded the city of Batavia on Java (today's Jakarta), just 20 years after the return of this first successful expedition to Amsterdam. It was the start of a multinational that would continue for two hundred years.

Around 1600, Amsterdam has no one to match the skill of Haarlem's Vroom as a painter of marines. It is hardly surprising that the patrons who commissioned this work, perhaps the very merchants who had fitted out the expedition portrayed here, chose the famous artist from the neighbouring city.

Gerrit Pietersz Sweelinck of Amsterdam specialised in painting biblical and mythological scenes and portraits. He was a teacher of Rembrandt's teacher, Pieter Lastman. This portrait shows his brother, the organist and composer Jan Pietersz Sweelinck, who was known throughout Europe. Their father, Jan Sywertszoon, had also been an organist at Amsterdam's Oude Kerk. After his death in 1580, his son Jan had followed in his footsteps and taken over his father's position. The post remained in the family after Jan's death too; he was followed by his son Dirk.

On weekdays, Jan Pietersz Sweelinck would play the organ in free concerts for the public which became enormously popular. His virtuosity on the organ earned him the nickname Orpheus on the Amstel, after the mythological figure known for his fine voice and lyre playing. The inscription *M.IO. Pet./.Swll.Ams.Or.* inside the oval, refers to this honorary title.

An interesting aspect of the painting is the subject's left hand that extends out of the painting's inner frame. This gives an even greater sense of depth to the portrait, so that the subject seems to be in the same room as we are.

JAN PIETERSZ SWEELINCK (1562-1621), 1606

Gerrit Pietersz Sweelinck
(Amsterdam 1566-after 1612 Amsterdam)

Panel 67.7 × 51.6 cm
Inscription and date left and top right of the oval:
Aetatis: 44 / an° 1606
On loan from the Gemeentemuseum, The Hague

Acts 14:8-18, in the New Testament, tells the story of St Paul and St Barnabas at Lystra. Paul has just healed a cripple who had been unable to walk since birth. The man can be seen behind the altar, holding a crutch. This miraculous cure has convinced the assembled crowd that the two apostles must be the gods Jupiter and Mercury. The priest of Jupiter at Lystra, dressed in white and wearing a laurel crown, is determined to sacrifice a white bull to the two apostles. 'When the apostles Barnabas and Paul heard this they rent their clothes, and ran in among the people, crying out and saying, Men, why do you these things? We also are men of like passions with you, and preach to you that you should turn from these vanities to the living God, who made heaven and earth and the sea, and all things that are therein.'

It is noticeable how often this theme appears in paintings at the time of the struggle between the moderate remonstrant and the strict counter-remonstrant factions in the Dutch Reformed Church. Paul and Barnabas presumably represent the moderates, while the crowd represents their opponents. The stricter faction managed to impose its will at the synod of Dort in 1618/19.

PAUL AND BARNABAS AT LYSTRA
1617

Pieter Lastman
(Amsterdam 1583-1633 Amsterdam)

Panel, 76 × 115 cm
Signed and dated on the base of the column:
Pietro lastman fc./ 1617

This painting by Cornelis van der Voort is the earliest surviving group portrait of governors of a charitable institution in Amsterdam. A rare record of the payment for this painting has also survived in the archives. 'This day, 10 November 1617, the governors of this hospital have each paid Master Cornelis van der Voort (from their own pocket) fifty guilders in cash for the portrayal of their persons, and three guilders each to Hans Hem for furnishing the frame, making in total three hundred and eighteen guilders … ƒ 318 to serve as a memorial to posterity and a defence against those who might suspect otherwise'.

Van der Voort arranged the governors around a table, examining the books for the rent of houses in the years 1617 and 1618. These accounts emphasise the administrative duties that the governors fulfilled, like the seals shown on the left. The charitable purpose of their institution is expressed in the painting on the wall seen through the corridor: it depicts Christ healing the lame.

GOVERNORS OF BINNEN-GASTHUIS HOSPITAL 1617-18

Cornelis van der Voort
(Antwerpen 1576-1624 Amsterdam)

Canvas, 197 × 239 cm
Monogrammed and dated below right:
Anno 1617 cvv f

According to a 1606 regulation, the lecturer of the Surgeons' Guild was required to teach osteology twice a week. This painting, attributed to Nicolaes Eliasz Pickenoy, shows a lesson on the structure and function of the skeleton by Dr Sebastiaen Egbertsz (1563-1621). He is the man wearing a hat and pointing to the humerus, the bone of the upper left arm. The skeleton probably belonged to an English pirate who had been executed. Egbertsz had dissected his corpse in 1615 in an anatomy lesson.

The names of the men portrayed are listed at the top left of the painting; some of the numbers correspond with those above the heads of the men in the portrait. From left to right, these are Lambert Jacobsz, Anthoni Jansz Uytdenhooven, Sebastiaen Egbertsz, Hendrick Claesz Koolvelt, Jan Arentsz de Wees and Gerrit Indies.

The symmetrical arrangement around the skeleton, the space given to each subject, and the lifelike pose and gesture of each of these men, combine to make this a highly successful group portrait.

THE OSTEOLOGY LESSON OF DR SEBASTIAEN EGBERTSZ
1619

Nicolaes Eliasz Pickenoy, attributed
(Amsterdam 1588-1650/56 Amsterdam)

Canvas, 135 × 186 cm

In 1578, Amsterdam came out in favour of the rebellion against the Spanish crown, much later than most of Holland's principal towns. Cornelis Pietersz Hooft, a republican sympathiser who had been forced to flee in 1569, was now able to return. That same year he married Anna Jacobsdr Blaeu. Here Cornelis van der Voort has portrayed the couple in old age. Their similar pose and dress, both wearing black gowns trimmed with brown fur, emphasise the unity of the two works.

Hooft was born north of Amsterdam in Zaanstreek and traded in oil, grain and herring on Nieuwendijk. When he returned from exile to Amsterdam, he went into politics, first as a councillor and a sheriff, then between 1588 and 1610 serving twelve terms as a burgomaster. His political influence then began to ebb as the conflict in the Dutch Reformed Church between the less stringent remonstrants and the far stricter counter-remonstrants gathered pace. Hooft supported the moderate remonstrants and found himself opposed by Gerrit Jacobsz Witsen. Having been forced out of politics, in 1611 he took a position as master of the Orphan Chamber.

Anna Blaeu, a cousin of Willem Jansz Blaeu (1571-1638), the famous cartographer (see p. 66), had migrated to Amsterdam from Antwerp. Pieter Cornelisz Hooft, the famous poet, was a son of the couple portrayed here.

CORNELIS PIETERSZ HOOFT
(1547-1626), 1622

Cornelis van der Voort
(Antwerp 1576-1624 Amsterdam)

Inscription and date, top right: Aetatis. *Suae. 76 Ann. 1622*
On loan from the Rijksmuseum, Amsterdam

ANNA JACOBSDR BLAEU
(1556-1627), 1622

Panel, 122 × 90 cm
Inscription and date, top left: *Aetatis. Suae.
66 Anno 1622*

The seventeenth century was in the middle of what has been termed the Little Ice Age. Many winters in this period were exceptionally harsh. The winter of 1620-21 was particularly cold, even for that time. The IJ froze over completely. That was unusual and is perhaps what prompted Cabel to paint this work. The artist portrayed the frozen waterfront from the north bank of the IJ, probably standing on Waterland dyke, between Nieuwendam and Buiksloot. In the distance, on the opposite side of the ice, lies Amsterdam's familiar profile (see p. 6).

A large crowd has gathered on the ice. Many of them are skating and walking across the ice towards Schreierstoren. Young and old, rich and poor; everyone seems to be on the ice. A rich young man in the foreground, in the centre, is looking directly at us, for example. His clothes contrast sharply with those of the man on the left gathering his nets. His torn coat will not have offered the fisherman much protection against the cold.

Cabel depicts all kinds of activity. Some people have ventured onto the ice to have fun, while many others are there to earn a living.

WINTER SCENE ON THE IJ AT AMSTERDAM
c. 1620-23

Arent Arentsz, called Cabel
(Amsterdam 1585/86-1631 Amsterdam)

Panel, 52.5 × 99 cm
Monogrammed below right,
on the side of the barrel: AA

Werner van den Valckert painted the civic guard company of district VIII in 1625. This precinct covered the area east of Nieuwmarkt, between Geldersekade and Oude Schans, north of Keizerstraat and south of Kromme Waal. Seated at the table are captain Albert Coenraetsz Burgh (1593-1647) and lieutenant Pieter Evertsz Hulft (1578-1638). Burgh is holding a compass, symbolically connecting a map of the district with a plan of a fortress. This gestures points to the militia company's duty to provide security for the area.

Second from the right, a man is holding a manual of military exercises: Jacques de Gheyn's *Wapenhandelinghe* (English edition: *Mars His Field or The Exercise of Armes*) which appeared in 1607 under the auspices of Prince Maurits. The militiamen would have used it as a practical guide for drill. The book is open, showing the first illustration in the section on pikemen.

The man standing in the centre is ensign Arent Willemsz van Buyl (d. 1646). The company's loyalty to the prince is evident from its standard, which sports Maurits's arms. Both Burgh and Hulft owed their appointment to the town council to Maurits. The stadholder died in 1625. It may have been his death that led to the commission for this portrait.

CIVIC GUARDSMEN OF THE COMPANY OF CAPTAIN ALBERT COENRAETSZ BURGH AND LIEUTENANT PIETER EVERTSZ HULFT 1625

Werner Jacobsz van den Valckert
(Amsterdam c. 1585-after 1635 Amsterdam)

Panel, 169.5 × 270 cm
Signed and dated lower right:
Warner v. Valckert f: 1625; dated on the chimneypiece: ANNO 1625

E ach year, a procession marched through Amsterdam's old east side on the first Monday after Epiphany and through the new west side the next day. These were the inmates of the Leper House, located on the outskirts of the city, who were permitted to collect money on that day. Copper Monday, as the day was known, was abolished by the burgomasters in 1604, since the procession attracted huge unruly crowds.

When Van Nieulandt painted his panorama of Dam Square in 1633, the procession was already a thing of the past.

Dam Square, with the old town hall on the left, forms the backdrop for the procession. The lepers are seated in sleighs, drawn across the square by horses. They attract people's attention by rattling their Lazarus clappers. The barrel is for the money collected, while a drummer heads the parade.

Although the lepers have drawn a large crowd, life on the square carries on as normal. A quacksalver is selling his wares on the right, while a group of officials from the madhouse march past him advertising the forthcoming lottery. The area around the weigh house and the start of the harbour at Damrak was a hub of commercial activity. In Van Nieulandt's view, the procession hardly interrupted the normal business at all. In fact it was just one of the many attractions on a Monday in January.

THE PROCESSION OF LEPERS ON COPPER MONDAY
1633

Adriaen van Nieulandt
(Antwerp 1587-1658 Amsterdam)

Signed and dated on the board in the foreground, right:
Adriaen / van Nieulandt / Fecit . 1633
Canvas, 212 × 308 cm

JAARLYKSE OMMEGANK DER LEPROOZEN. OP COPPERTIES MAANDAG OPGEHOUDE IN JAAR 1604

BANQUET OF CIVIC GUARDSMEN OF THE COMPANY OF CAPTAIN JACOB BACKER AND LIEUTENANT JACOB ROGH

1632-34

Nicolaes Eliasz Pickenoy
(Amsterdam 1588-1650/56 Amsterdam)

Canvas, 198 × 531 cm

Between 1623 and 1633, the crossbow civic guard renovated and expanded their headquarters on Singel canal, which created more space for new group portraits. Three paintings had already been commissioned before 1630 (see p. 38). Another four were to follow, including two from Pickenoy.

It is interesting that Nicolaes Pickenoy chose to use the banquet motif for his group portrait. The theme had not been employed in Amsterdam since 1613. He was probably inspired in part by the work of Frans Hals of Haarlem. Hals had recently produced a series of convincing group portraits of civic guards at table. Hals's influence is also discernable in the way Pickenoy brings life to his portrait by varying the direction of his subjects' gaze.

The portrait shows the men of district IX, the area north of Nieuwmarkt. Seated at the head of the table on the left, is captain Jacob Backer (1572-1643), who stood down in 1632 to become a burgomaster, which may have been the occasion that prompted this portrait. Sitting to the right of Backer is Jacob Rogh (1586-1670), the company's lieutenant. The ensign, standing prominently in front of the table, is Roelof Bicker (1611-1656).

This painting shows the men of district XVIII, the area between Rokin and Nieuwezijds Achterburgwal (today's Spuistraat). Almost all of the 21 men are standing in one long line, which accounts for the unusual shape of the portrait. It is also noticeable that almost all the subjects are looking directly at us.

The somewhat older man with the beard, left of the ensign, is captain Jacob Symonsz de Vries. Like Thomas de Keyser, he was a remonstrant and indeed a close friend of the artist. It is hardly surprising that De Keyser was commissioned to paint De Vries's civic guard company.

An interesting detail is the glimpse into the room behind the hall in which the men are gathered. There are two figures in the room, playing dice on a drum. This was a popular motif in genre paintings of the time.

Besides De Vries, only lieutenant Dirck de Graeff has been identified. He is sitting to the right of the ensign. De Graeff was a member of a prominent Amsterdam family. This may be why he, though a lieutenant, is holding the commander's baton that would normally be held by the captain.

CIVIC GUARDSMEN OF THE COMPANY OF CAPTAIN JACOB SYMONSZ DE VRIES AND LIEUTENANT DIRCK DE GRAEFF

1633

Thomas de Keyser
(Amsterdam 1596-1667 Amsterdam)

Canvas, 198 × 604 cm
Monogrammed and dated on the wall above the passage:
TDK ANNO 1633

GOVERNESSES OF THE CIVIC ORPHANAGE
1634

Jacob Adriaensz Backer
(Harlingen 1608-1651 Amsterdam)

Canvas, 238 × 274 cm
Signed above the door, right: *J A. Backer*
On loan from Spirit, Amsterdam

This painting, which still hangs on the wall for which it was intended, was seen in the eighteenth century by Jan Wagenaar, in the same place. 'One of the governess portraits, by Jacob Backer, is particularly noted for its realism and art,' he wrote in his description of Amsterdam. A recent restoration of the work has made these qualities all the more evident.

In the composition, the light enters from the right, which is unusual in a work by Backer. It seems that Backer may have taken account of the way the light entered the room in which the painting was to hang - also from the right. A surviving receipt for the canvas on which Backer portrayed the governesses shows that the work was completed in 1634. On 7 December 1633, Anthony Besaer received payment for a canvas 'on which the governesses shall be depicted'. The portrait may have been prompted by the renovation of the girl's wing.

The painting shows four women, the governesses of the Civic Orphanage, at a table in an imaginary room. The surviving list of governesses enables us to identify the women in the picture, from left to right: Dieuwertje Bicker (1584-1641), Annetge Backer (1572-1639), Aechje Oetgens van Waveren (1566-1639) and Aegen Francken (1572-1651). There is an inkstand and a quill on the table beside a volume that may be the children's book in which the orphans were registered. The woman behind the table who has just brought a young orphan into the room is the orphanage matron. The girl is wearing the orphanage's red-and-black uniform. Other painters after Backer also embellished their portraits of governors and governesses by including a child being ushered into the room (see p. 8 and 58). The orphanage offered shelter to the children of *poorters*, townsmen with the status and rights of a burgher. Other orphans were taken up by the almoners orphanage.

Backer was one of the first artists to paint a group portrait in which he showed his subjects full length. His virtuosity as an artist is evident in the wrinkled skin of the hands and faces of the old governesses and their black, fur-trimmed gowns.

In 1615, Gerbrand Bredero (1585-1615) wrote a farce called *Moortje*. In the play, Mooy-Aeltje, a girl from a poor family, is forced to choose between the old, but rich captain Roemert and the handsome, young Ritsaert, who constantly finds himself without a penny. In the end, Kackerlack has a solution for Mooy-Aeltje. She chooses both: staying with one and then the other in turn. In the painting, Roemert shows off his wealth, while Ritsaert points to the reason why he never has any money: his glass.

Moeyaert did not paint a specific scene in the play; the principal characters even never appear on stage together. Instead, he created a visual summary of the piece, thereby emphasising its moralistic quality. The theme, the choice between old and rich or young and poor, often appears in works by seventeenth-century Dutch artists.

In 1637, seven performances of *Moortje* were staged by the Eglentier *rederijkers* or theatrical society. They had premises on the floor above the meat market (Kleine Vleeshal) on Nes. Moeyaert had been a member of the society since 1618. Perhaps it was the production of the play that prompted the painting. Moeyaert's focus on the theatrical characters and the pronounced contrast of light and shade are reminiscent of Caravaggio and his followers in Utrecht.

MOOY-AEL AND HER SUITORS
c. 1638

Nicolaes Moeyaert
(Amsterdam c. 1590/91-1655 Amsterdam)

Canvas, 113 × 126.7 cm
Monogram, amended to a signature (false), centre left: GL. Metsu
Inscription the girl's collar: *Mooy: aeltgen*
On loan from the Rijksmuseum, Amsterdam

Dirck Jacobsz Bas (1569-1637) served twelve terms as a burgomaster of Amsterdam. He was born into a family of exiles in Emden. After studying in Leiden, Heidelberg, Padua, Siena and Basel, he settled in Amsterdam, where he won a seat on the town council in 1600. He must have been an accomplished diplomat, since he was often sent on missions abroad. In the centre of this portrait, Dirck Bas is seated on a chair beside his second wife, Margriet Snoeck (1588-1645). Standing on the left is Abraham de Visscher and his wife Machteld Bas, Dirck's daughter. In front of them, with a dog, is their son. Behind Dirck Bas is his eldest son Jacob Dircksz Bas. The young man on the right is his youngest son, Nicolaes Bas, who died not long after Santvoort's portrait was completed, at La Rochelle while travelling through Europe. He is flanked by his two sisters, Agatha (left) and Lysbeth (right). In the eighteenth century, coats of arms and names were added above each of the figures at the top of the painting. By then the son's name was apparently forgotten. He was Abraham junior, born in 1633. In fact, his portrait may have been added some years later.

DIRCK JACOBSZ BAS AND HIS FAMILY
c. 1635

Dirck Dircksz van Santvoort
(Amsterdam 1610-1680 Amsterdam)

Canvas, 136 × 251 cm
On loan from the Rijksmuseum, Amsterdam

Jan Cornelisz Geelvinck, merchant and shipowner, looks us in the eye, proud and confident. This portrait by Jonson van Ceulen is a rather traditional half-length figure against a plain background, with a pair of gloves held in the left hand as the only attribute.

At the time of this painting, Geelvinck was serving his eleventh term as a burgomaster of the city. He had cemented his position in Amsterdam's patrician elite through his marriage to Agatha de Vlaming van Oudtshoorn. His links with the influential and powerful Bicker family probably also helped him attain the post of burgomaster. In 1639, Geelvinck's daughter Eva married Hendrick Bicker (see p. 47).

Jonson van Ceulen, a portrait painter originally from London, worked for a few years in Amsterdam around 1650. His portrait of Geelvinck shows the influence of Anthony van Dyck. Geelvinck's daughter and son-in-law had also chosen this courtly style when they commissioned Von Sandrart to paint their portraits seven years earlier. The style became increasingly fashionable in the second half of the seventeenth century.

JAN CORNELISZ GEELVINCK (1579-1651), 1646

Cornelis Jonson van Ceulen
(London 1593-1661 Utrecht)

Canvas, 85 × 71.5 cm
Signed bottom left: **Corns Jonson Londonus fecit.**
Date and inscription top left: *Anno Dom 1646 / AEtatis Suae 67*

In 1639 Hendrik Bicker, a member of the influential Bicker family, married Eva Geelvinck, daughter of Jan Cornelisz Geelvinck (see opposite), who served twelve terms as burgomaster. To mark the wedding, two portraits were commissioned from Joachim von Sandrart, a native of Frankfurt. The family commissioned several portraits from Von Sandrart: the artist also painted Hendrick's brother Jacob and second cousin Alida Bicker, as well as a group portrait of Cornelis Bicker's civic guard company.

Having travelled across Europe, Von Sandrart knew many personalities in the international art world. From 1637 to 1642, he worked in Amsterdam. His wide experience is evident in these portraits. The young couple are depicted in three-quarter length portraits against a curtain, with a park landscape in the background. This was new in Amsterdam. It shows the influence of Anthony van Dyck, who worked at the British court. It was not until the late 1640s that this type of portrait became genuinely popular in Amsterdam, with artists such as Flinck, Bol and Van der Helst.

Von Sandrart's unfamiliar style of painting and the critical comments he wrote about Rembrandt in his *Teutsche Academie* earned him a marginal place in the Dutch artistic pantheon. Yet in recent years Von Sandrart has won many admirers among those who now recognise his qualities as a skilled, significant and innovative portrait painter.

HENDRICK BICKER
(1615-1651), 1639

Joachim von Sandrart
(Frankfurt 1606-1688 Nuremberg)

Canvas, 139 × 105 cm
Signed and dated on the arm of the chair,
right: *J. Sandrart / 1639*

EVA GEELVINCK
(1619-1698), 1639

Canvas, 139 × 105 cm
Signed and dated, below left: *J. Sandrart / f. 1639*

Having lived for around ten years in Rome, Bartholomeus Breenbergh returned to Amsterdam in 1630, where he married Rebecca Schellingwou in 1633. In 1644, Jacob Backer painted their portraits. Joachim von Sandrart, who wrote a biography of artists, praised Backer for the virtuosity and astonishing speed with which he painted. Von Sandrart witnessed for himself that a woman came from Haarlem to have her portrait painted by Backer, and was able to return home that same day with the completed painting.

These portraits also show the artist's skilful use of the brush, for example in the superbly rendered fan that Rebecca is holding in her right hand. Backer painted both husband and wife *all'antica*: in fantasy costumes intended to evoke associations with classical antiquity. This style of portrait was one of Backer's specialities and particularly suitable for a portrait of an artist who had spent so many years in Rome and who himself painted historical scenes inspired by Italy's past. The work seems to advertise Breenbergh as a man of expertise in the Italian Renaissance and classical history.

BARTHOLOMEUS BREENBERGH (1598-1657), 1644

Jacob Adriaensz Backer
(Harlingen 1608-1651 Amsterdam)

Canvas, 93 × 72 cm
Monogrammed and dated, bottom right: JAB / 1644

REBECCA SCHELLINGWOU (1610-1667), 1644

Canvas, 93.5 × 72.5 cm
Monogrammed bottom left: JAB

This three-year-old boy, in his remarkable red coat, is Hiob de Wildt. Van Santvoort portrayed the boy, as well as his parents David de Wildt (1611-1671) and Elisabeth van der Voorde (1611-1677) in 1640. A year later, Hiob's father was appointed to the prominent position of secretary to the Amsterdam admiralty.

The family's status is emphasised in the portrait by the boy's bow and arrow. Hunting was still an aristocratic privilege at that time. Here Van Santvoort presents Hiob as part of the absolute elite. The black dog Hiob has by a leash may symbolise hunting as well, although it may also be a commentary on how young boys should be raised. Johan van Beverwijck, a Dordrecht physician, wrote on discipline and the raising of children. 'Just like horses [...] if boys are not trained and properly educated their speech will always be rough and they will never listen to discipline: it is the same with children, if one gives a child free rein and lets it grow up wild.' Perhaps this allusion to a bridled horse can be extended to the dog on its leash, so that Hiob is portrayed here as a boy who is being raised properly.

HIOB DE WILDT
(1637-1704), 1640

Dirck Dircksz van Santvoort
(*Amsterdam 1610-1680 Amsterdam*)

Canvas, 123.5 × 91 cm
Signed and dated below, centre:
D. D. Santvoort fe. / 1640
On loan from Netherlands Institute for Cultural Heritage

Govert Flinck, *Study for
a Civic Guard Portrait*, 1648.
Canvas, 66.7 × 101.6 cm

CIVIC GUARDS OF THE COMPANY OF CAPTAIN JOAN HUYDECOPER AND LIEUTENANT FRANS VAN WAVEREN
1648

Govert Flinck
(Kleve 1615-1660 Amsterdam)

Canvas, 265 × 513 cm
Signed and dated below, left: *Flinck f 1648*

Govert Flinck was one of Amsterdam's leading portrait artists in the 1640s. He was commissioned to paint this work in 1648. A note which Govert Flinck included in the painting, below in the centre, and which is now illegible, once showed a verse by Jacob Vos.

> Thus Van Maarsseveen
> leads us to a lasting peace,
> Just as his father led us
> fighting for the state;
> Wisdom and courage,
> the strength of a free city,
> Dispel that ancient grudge,
> replace the battle dress.
> Now they stand guard on the Y,
> the killing and pillage are done,
> For wise men lay their sword
> to rest, but not to rust.

The portly figure in black on the left in the foreground is Captain Joan Huydecoper van Maarsseveen (1599-1661), a member of a wealthy patrician family in Amsterdam, who served six terms as a burgomaster. Jan Vos refers in his verse to Huydecoper's father, Jan Bal, who lived in exile during the Dutch Revolt and commanded troops in the war. Now, following the Treaty of Munster, Huydecoper himself leads the way to peace. The verse places particular emphasis on the captain of the militia unit, which suggests that it may have been his idea to commission the group portrait. This is perhaps confirmed by the building in the background: that is the house on Singel canal built by Philips Vingboons around 1640 for Huydecoper. It was destroyed in 1943 when a British plane crashed into it.

Among the other men depicted in the portrait, Lieutenant Frans Oetgens van Waveren (1619-1659) is shown taking off his hat to Huyde-coper and presenting the men, while Nicolaes Oetgens van Waveren, Frans's brother, is the ensign.

Flinck painted a preparatory study for this painting, the only sketch for a group portrait of civic guards to survive. It provides unique testimony to the history of the portrait. Flinck made significant changes to the composition before painting the final version. He created more distance between the two groups, perhaps to provide space for Huydecoper's house.

Flinck also added his own portrait, behind the captain, to the right.

TWO GOVERNORS AND TWO GOVERNESSES OF THE WORKHOUSE (SPINHUIS)

1650

Bartholomeus van der Helst
(Haarlem c. 1613-1670 Amsterdam)

Canvas, 233 × 317 cm
Dated, centre right on the book: *Alphabet Anno 1650*

In 1598, Amsterdam set up a workhouse: called Spinhuis. An inscription on the doorway declared: 'To teach humble girls, maidens and women to avoid indolence, deviance and beggary [...]'. In other words, a house of correction for women, a place to rehabilitate criminals, beggars and prostitutes. On 18 February 1643, the building on Oudezijds Voorburgwal was destroyed by fire; a new building was erected on the same site and in 1645 convicted women were once again admitted. Five years later, Bartholomeus van der Helst was commissioned to paint this portrait.

Four governors and two governesses ran the institution. The two oldest governors had been involved in the reconstruction of the building. To judge from the probable age of the men depicted here, these must be the two youngest governors. They are Jacob van Rijn and Nicolaes Rochusz van de Capelle, the former being the latter's junior by eleven years and presumably therefore the man furthest to the right. The two governesses are Catharina Brouwers (behind the table) and Pietertje de Vries (in front of the table).

The governors and governesses  are seated around a table. The man on the right is looking directly at us, gesturing with his hand as if saying something. The other three are deep in conversation about some matter or other. The governor is showing a document, while the governess is about to write in her book. In the scene, they are portrayed as concerned governors and governesses administering the institution's finances. To the right, a man is approaching carrying a large volume from an adjacent room. The volume's title is *Alphabet Anno 1650*. Perhaps it is a register of admissions to the workhouse.

In the background, behind the main figures, the daily routine of the workhouse continues. One of the women is being beaten with a shoe. The scene is well suited to P.C. Hooft's motto for the institution, inscribed above the new doorway. 'Fear not, I do not avenge, but compel to the good / My hand is harsh but my heart is loving'. Corporal punishment was apparently an integral part of rehabilitation and education. The men to the right of the wooden partition have paid two *stuivers* to witness the spectacle. At that time, the workhouse was a major attraction.

In the night of 4 to 5 March 1651, a northwesterly storm raged over Amsterdam, just when the spring tide was at its height. The growing swell of water that became known as St Peter's flood, had calamitous consequences. A dyke burst in two places east of Amsterdam: the spectacular breaching of Sint Anthonis or Diemen dyke was portrayed by various artists. In addition to several drawings and etchings of the event, Willem Schellinks also painted this work. This breach in the dyke happened near Houtewael, a village then just east of Amsterdam, roughly where today's Sarphatistraat meets Hoogte Kadijk. Schellinks suggests Amsterdam's proximity by the three church towers and one or two ships' masts, rather nearer than they would have been in reality.

Overamstel polder and the newly reclaimed Diemermeer were flooded. Jan Wagenaar described the results around 1760: 'De Meer found itself under sixteen foot of water. All the plantations and several summer houses were destroyed. The following year, their proprietors were forced to visit these parks and pleasure gardens by barge.' Happily for the unfortunate owners, the damage was repaired within a few years.

THE BREACHING OF SINT ANTHONISDIJK AT HOUTEWAEL IN 1651
c. 1651-55

Willem Schellinks
(Amsterdam 1627-1678 Amsterdam)

Canvas, 47 × 68 cm
Loan from Stichting Genootschap Amsterdams
Historisch Museum

Four months after the flood that broke Sint Anthonisdijk at Houtewael (see opposite), another disaster struck. A review of the year's events in the *Hollantse Mercurius* described it as follows: 'On 7 July at two o'clock in the night, the old Town Hall of Amsterdam caught fire, near the tower.' It was not just the tower; in the end, the entire complex lay in ruins. Yet few people in Amsterdam felt any remorse at the loss of the building, as the writer in *Hollantse Mercurius* noted. 'The destruction was welcomed since it saved the cost of knocking it down.' In 1648, work had already begun on a new Town Hall. The scaffolding can be seen behind the weigh house on the far right. The old structure consumed by flames in this painting had already been earmarked for demolition.

Little of the city's sanguine attitude is evident in Beertstraaten's dramatic account. Many have gathered on Dam Square to try and put the fire out, to protect the adjacent buildings and to rescue items from inside the Town Hall. Buckets of water are handed through from Damrak to the Town Hall. Wet blankets are hanging from gabled roofs at the start of Kalverstraat.

THE BURNING OF THE OLD TOWN HALL ON DAM SQUARE IN 1652
c. 1652-55

Jan Abrahamsz Beerstraaten
(*Amsterdam 1622-1666 Amsterdam*)

Canvas, 89 × 121.8 cm
Signed, left on the sluice: *BEERSTRATEN*

'I close this day a cycle of six times eleven years, / And see my head snow-capped, and count the grey hairs,/ Though without my glass eye, in this painting,/ And still my heart lights up in lust for poetry;/ As I teach Lucifer to play his tragedian's part,/ And strike lightning on celestial stages,/ To shock and mirror Ambition and Envy./ What is my age? Smoke, damp; not time.' Joost van den Vondel wrote this when he saw his portrait by Govert Flinck. The poet and playwright, who turned 66 on 17 November 1653, completed his tragedy *Lucifer* in 1654, about the fallen angel who rebelled against God. The play did not earn Vondel much success. It was banned by the burgomasters after two performances, when Protestant clergymen complained that it mixed religious and secular elements. This was considered too Catholic. To make matters worse, two years later, the stocking shop which Vondel had inherited from his father went bankrupt. For the rest of his life he made his living in the rather mediocre position of bookkeeper at the city's lending bank.

By contrast, Govert Flinck's career was reaching a crescendo in 1653; he received major commissions from the city to provide paintings for the new Town Hall that opened in 1655. Unfortunately, he died before completing all the planned works. Vondel retired in 1668 and survived Flinck by many years.

JOOST VAN DEN VONDEL (1587-1679), 1653

Govert Flinck
(Kleve 1615-1660 Amsterdam)

Canvas, 42.5 × 38 cm
On loan from the Rijksmuseum, Amsterdam

We are looking down on Amsterdam, from hundreds of metres in the sky. Micker took an extremely unusual vantage point for his view of the city. Moreover, this is not what Amsterdam looked like in the seventeenth century. This is a view of the city as it would have appeared around 1540. Micker based his composition on the sixteenth-century painting by Cornelis Anthonisz and a print of that work (see p. 26-27). It may have been Micker who restored the panel when it was damaged in the fire at the old Town Hall (see p. 55). Areas of the seventeenth-century

restoration on the original match Micker's canvas.

Micker depicted Amsterdam as if there were clouds in the sky: parts of the city are in shade, other parts are in sunlight. Dam Square, with the old Town Hall and Nieuwe Kerk, is basking in sunshine in the centre of the painting. Damrak, which is full of boats and, further down, the Oude Kerk, are half in shadow.

Below left lies Schreierstoren, which was then still part of the town wall. Further left is the harbour area with its many unfinished vessels at the shipyard.

BIRD'S-EYE VIEW OF AMSTERDAM
in or after 1652

Jan Micker
(Amsterdam 1598/1600-1664 Amsterdam)

Canvas, 100 × 137 cm
Signed bottom right on the legend: *IMicker fecit*

The Leper House was originally a medieval institution, a leper colony in which people suffering from leprosy lived in isolation. Until the sixteenth century, the leper house was located outside Amsterdam's town walls, where today's Meester Visserplein is. After 1600, the city expanded steadily and the house was soon absorbed, by which time leprosy had become a rare disease. The Leper House had also begun catering for other patients. The boy being led in to see the governors has a fungal infection on his head. It was common at the time and was known as favus or scald-head. His malady confirms that other diseases were also treated at the leper house. The boy is clutching a *vuylbrief*, an official

permit to enable him to enter the leper house. The governors sitting around the table are, from right to left, Jacob Willem Hooft (1586- 1685), Augustijn Wtenbogaert (1577-1655), Pieter Cleutrijn (1585/90-after 1651) and Joan van Hartoghvelt (1602-1669). The boy's purpose in the composition is to show the governors as benefactors. This same motif appears in the earlier portraits for the Civic Orphanage (see p. 8 and 58). In fact the Leper House was not specifically for children. Apparently Bol decided that a sick child would garner more sympathy than a needy adult. At the same time, the work portrays the governors as charitable individuals, rather than just efficient administrators.

THE GOVERNORS OF THE LEPER HOUSE
1649

Ferdinand Bol
(Dordrecht 1616-1680 Amsterdam)

Canvas, 224 × 310 cm
Signed and dated on the book above the inkpot:
f Bol fec./ 1649

After the Treaty of Munster in 1648, demand for group portraits of civic guards declined. The prestige associated with appearing in a portrait as a defender of the city had evaporated. The civic guard paintings of this period show none of the men, only the governors in charge of the headquarters. And they are not depicted in heroic poses, but as well-to-do administrators, as in this group portrait by Bartholomeus van der Helst. He portrayed these governors seated around a table discussing a stack of letters.

Shown between the two central governors is a man with an inkpot and quill. This is the innkeeper of the Crossbow Civic Guard, Christoffel Poock (1602-1661). His name is on the inkpot. His prominence in the portrait and the attributes he and one of the governors are holding - the inkpot and the letter – refer to a legal dispute that the governors had just won.

As innkeeper of the crossbowmen's guild, Poock was required to pay an annual contribution of 200 guilders to the Almoners House. Since the inn keepers at the other civic guard guilds did not have to pay anything, the governors sued. In 1656, the court in Amsterdam decided that the guild could buy off the obligation with a one-off payment of 500 guilders.

THE GOVERNORS OF THE CROSSBOW CIVIC GUARD 1656

Bartholomeus van der Helst
(Haarlem c. 1613-1670 Amsterdam)

Canvas, 183 × 254 cm
Signed and dated below right:
B. vander. helst. fecit 1656

In January 1656, Rembrandt was commissioned to paint a second anatomical lesson. He had already portrayed Dr Nicolaes Tulp and a group of surgeons in 1632. This time, the group portrait would feature a demonstration of dissection by Dr Jan Deyman (1619-1666).

The figure at the centre of this painting is the corpse of the executed Joris Fonteijn (1633/34-1656). His convincingly fores-hortened body, brightly illuminated from above, appears to jut out of the painting. The famous British artist

Joshua Reynolds remarked in 1781, 'There is something sublime in the character of the head which reminds me of Michael Angelo; the whole is finely painted, the colouring much like Titian.' Beside the dissecting table, holding the severed top of the skull, is the surgeon Gijsbert Calkoen (1621-1664), who assisted in the anatomy lesson. The hands holding up the membrane separating the two halves of the brain - the *falx cerebri* - belong to the lecturer, Jan Deyman. He is apparently preparing to expose the central section of the brain. The

THE ANATOMY LESSON OF DR JAN DEYMAN
1656

Rembrandt van Rijn
(Leiden 1606-1669 Amsterdam)

Canvas, 100 × 134 cm
Signed, left on the dissecting table: *Rembrandt f. 1656*

Rembrandt van Rijn, *The Anatomy Lesson of Dr Joan Deyman*, c. 1656. Pen and brush with grey and black ink, light wash, 110 × 133 mm

cortex of the two halves of the brain is clearly recognisable. From the empty void where the abdomen should be, it seems that Deyman had already completed the anatomy of this area before moving on to the head.

In 1656, Rembrandt was having considerable trouble keeping ahead of his creditors. The First Anglo-Dutch War (1652-54) had seriously damaged his financial position, after a decade in which he had only just managed to keep up his production of paintings. So the 500 guilders this commission paid would have been particularly welcome. Yet in the end, even this was not enough; on 10 July 1656 Rembrandt was forced to declare bankruptcy after all.

Originally, the canvas was around 245 by 300 centimetres. In 1723, most of the painting was lost in a fire in the guild room at the surgeons' guild, at the Weigh House on Nieuwmarkt. A drawing by Rembrandt himself shows what the painting would have looked like. Besides Deyman, his assistant and the anatomical subject, there were once another seven figures in the painting. From the drawing it seems that the surgeons were portrayed in a variety of poses and facing different directions. A figure on the far left is looking straight at us, while the figure on the right is focusing on what is happening around the dissecting table.

In 1841, the surgeon's widows' fund sold the surviving fragment to a London art dealer. Forty years later, the art historian Jan Six VII found it at the depot of London's South Kensington Museum. An appeal was launched and the work was purchased for the city of Amsterdam.

DAM SQUARE WITH THE TOWN HALL UNDER CONSTRUCTION 1656

Johannes Lingelbach
(Frankfurt a. M. 1622-1674 Amsterdam)

Canvas, 122.5 × 206 cm
Signed and dated, bottom left: *I: LINGELBACH. fecit 1656*

When fire destroyed the old Town Hall in 1652 (see p.55), work on its replacement had already begun. The ruins of the old municipal building were removed to make way for the new structure. This painting shows the new Town Hall under on the left. Since Dam Square was now considerably larger, Lingelbach was able to choose a position from which he could see both the Nieuwe Kerk and new Tow Hall on the left. To the right he shows Damrak, and the Oude Kerk tower looming high above the houses behind. On the far right is Huis onder 't Zeil and the fish market. In the centre of the square stands the Weigh House. Lingelbach depicted it at a slight angle to its actual position, placing it parallel to the facade of the new Town Hall.

When he painted this work, Lingelbach had just returned from Italy after a stay of several years. Back in Amsterdam, he painted numerous views of Italian cities. This specialisation is reflected in the painting here, with Dam Square bathed in a Mediterranean light. This southern atmosphere gives Amsterdam an almost Italian feel.

The square is bustling with activity, but unlike the scene on Copper Monday depicted by Van Nieulandt (see p.39) there is no sign of any poor or sickly Amsterdammers. The people milling around the square are affluent burghers and merchants, a surprising number of whom are removing their hat and politely greeting each other. In addition to the Italian atmosphere, the international feel of the painting is increased by the various exotic figures in the painting. A group of men from the Orient can be seen on the far right. To the left, a man who appears Spanish has raised his hat.

In general, Lingelbach did not produce an accurate picture of Amsterdam; this is a view of the city as it wanted to see itself: a commercial hub of international stature in which a building would soon rise that would justly deserve the predicate of eighth wonder of the world. We no longer know who commissioned this work, yet the patron was surely a proud Amsterdammer.

Not everything in the painting is equally grandiose. In front of the Town Hall construction site is the temporary office of the law court. A notice above the door of the wooden structure beside it announces the grim news: '896 dead'. This is the latest statistic for the epidemic of plague that raged at the time.

This *trompe l'oeil* by Cornelis Brisé is one of the first in the genre of optical illusion that developed in Dutch art in the 1650s. The work was painted for the Thesaurie Ordinaris at the new Town Hall. This was the treasury, where the city's finances were administered. The subject, a still life of documents, seals and bags of money was therefore particularly appropriate. Vondel, the poet (see p. 56), praised the painting. 'Look at that scene. What do you see up there? Papers, orders and letters, or do appearances deceive the eye?'

The receipts, drawings and seals are tied together and arranged in eight categories on the wall. Each of the cards provides a category, from left to right: Travel costs / Trials / Public works / Extraordinary receipts; below: Ordinary wages / Receipts for major excises / Land purchases / Fuel. In the treasury office itself, the painting rested on a table, thus making the illusion all the more effective.

When the Town Hall became a Royal Palace in 1808, the painting moved along with the administration to new premises at Prinsenhof on Oudezijds Voorburgwal. In 1906 it was displayed at the Stedelijk Museum and from there it came to the Amsterdam Historical Museum. In 1996, the work returned to the room for which it was originally intended, and can now normally be seen in the former Thesaurie Ordinaris at the Royal Palace on Dam Square.

DOCUMENTS RELATING TO THE TREASURY
1656

Cornelis Brisé
(Haarlem 1617-1665 Amsterdam)

Canvas, 194 × 250 cm
Signed twice, below right: *C. Brize f.*/ *1656* and below
right on a note: *Cornelis Brize*
Royal Palace Amsterdam
On loan from the Amsterdam Historical Museum

Jürgen Ovens worked in Amsterdam for two periods before returning for good to his native Holstein in 1663. His last major commission in Amsterdam was this group portrait for the civic orphanage, that can still be seen today in the room for which it was originally intended. Abraham de Vries and Jacob Backer had already painted group portraits for the governors' boardroom at the orphanage in the 1630s (see p. 42-43).

This portrait of the six governors may have been painted to mark the departure of Jacob Trip (1627-1670), the third man from the right.

Ovens, like De Vries and Backer, includes a reference to the charitable work of the depicted governors by portraying the admission of new orphans to the institution. The polite young boy in front of the table has just been registered. Not only is he well-dressed, the book he is holding and the hat which he has removed indicate a proper upbringing. The more shabbily dressed children to the left are also about to be registered. The child entering through the doorway may already be a resident of the orphanage; the boy is wearing the red-and-black uniform worn by the orphans. Behind the governors, the secretary is bringing a large volume which may be the register of the orphanage's children or *Kinderboek*.

THE GOVERNORS OF THE CIVIC ORPHANAGE 1663

Jürgen Ovens
(Tönning 1623-1678 Friedrichstadt a.d. Eider)

Canvas, 257 × 401 cm
Signed and dated below left on the note:
J.Ovens f.a. 1663
On loan from Spirit, Amsterdam

Joan Willemsz Blaeu was the son of the famous cartographer Willem Jansz Blaeu, who manufactured globes and published maps. Joan studied at Leiden and Padua, graduating in law. In 1634, he married Geertruyd Pietersdr Vermeulen. After his father's death in 1638, Joan Blaeu took over the globe and map business, together with his brother Cornelis. The company flourished. The Blaeus became the largest publishers of maps in Europe. Their finest achievement came in 1662 when they produced a collection of around 600 maps in an extremely expensive edition of between nine and twelve volumes (depending on the language of the edition) entitled *Atlas Maior*. Blaeu's main print workshop was on Gravenstraat, it had nine presses and was called Negen Muzen. This studio was lost in a fire in 1672. Although the company managed to continue, its heyday had passed. The next year Joan died and left the company to his son, Joan Jr.

Besides making maps and globes, Blaeu also served in public office. He was a member of the city council from 1651 to 1672 and one of the governors of the Longbow Civic Guard that Van der Helst portrayed in 1653. It is interesting that Blaeu preferred the rather obscure Jan van Rossum from Vianen to one of Amsterdam's more prominent portraitists, such as Bol or Van der Helst.

JOAN WILLEMSZ BLAEU (1596-1673), 1663

Jan van Rossum
(active in Vianen 1654-1678)

Canvas, 101 × 83.5 cm
Signed and dated on the column base:
J. van Rossum. fc. / 1663

GEERTRUYD PIETERSDR VERMEULEN (d. 1676), 1663

Canvas, 101 × 83.5 cm
Signed and dated below left, above the table:
J. v. Rossum. fc./ 1663

Reinier Nooms, though principally a painter of marines and harbour views, also produced a number of cityscapes in which water also played a significant part. In fact it is noticeable that this work includes no buildings of any significance. This is Prinsengracht, viewed from the bridge at Westermarkt and Rozengracht, looking south towards Reesluis.

On the right is a barge from Leiden, identifiable by the keys in the flag. Perhaps it was delivering produce for the vegetable market that was held on this quay. The raised sails may have been added to provide an animated element to the composition, although bargemen often dried their sails in this way.

On the right, a woman is washing clothes in the canal. At the bridge, on the left, stands a cabin with the sign of a red stag. This was the emblem of the Roode Hert brewery which was not far from here. The cloths hanging to dry on the railing along the bridge are probably sacks that were used for cooking hops.

The mill in the distance is a post mill. This stood on one of the bulwarks along the town wall. When the city began to extend its ring of canals again in 1662, the bulwark and the mill were both demolished.

PRINSENGRACHT AT REESLUIS
c. 1663-64

Reinier Nooms, known as Zeeman
(Amsterdam 1623/24-1664 Amsterdam)

Canvas, 52 × 67 cm
Signed on the building on the canalside, right: *R. Zeeman*

In 1662, Amsterdam adopted the plan for a Fourth Expansion that would complete the city's characteristic semicircular arrangement of canals. For Berchem, this was an opportunity to sing the praises of the growing city in an allegorical painting.

The woman wearing a white gown and holding a map is the personification of Amsterdam. At her feet, river gods personify the Amstel and the IJ. Further to the left we see Neptune. The female figure on the shell holding a cornucopia is Plenty. Berchem's allegory suggests that Amsterdam's prosperity comes through overseas trade and is due to its location on the Amstel and IJ.

Leaning further right is Minerva, symbol of wisdom, and behind her is Truth. Amsterdam is looking up to the father of the gods, Jupiter, and his wife Juno, who has descended from her chariot drawn by peacocks. Other Olympic deities are also recognisable further in the background, on the right. High above, Fame declaims Amsterdam's name to all points of the compass, symbolised by the cherubs blowing in each direction. Behind this group is Iris, Juno's messenger, who announces Amsterdam's greatness to the universe.

The map that Amsterdam is holding is the plan by Daniël Stalpaert showing the projected expansion of the city.

Nicolaes Berchem supplied various allegorical figures for this map, published by Nicolaes Visscher II (1648-1702). In 1711, a German traveler, Zacharias Conrad von Uffenbach, reported seeing an *Allegory* by Berchem in Visscher's print shop: 'In another room we saw a piece representing the city of Amsterdam, painted by Van Berghem.'

It is tempting to see Visscher as the patron who commissioned this work, although it is quite possible that the *Allegory* Von Uffenbach saw was a different work altogether.

ALLEGORY OF THE EXPANSION OF AMSTERDAM
c. 1663

Nicolaes Berchem
(Haarlem 1620-1683 Amsterdam)

Canvas, 172.5 × 148 cm
Signed below left: *NBerchem f*

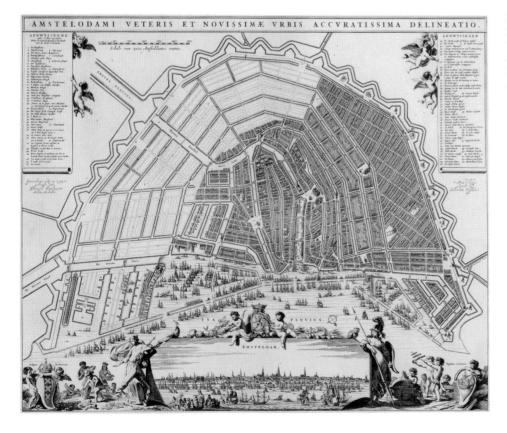

Daniël Stalpaert (1615-1670), published by Nicolaes Visscher (1618-1679), *Map of Amsterdam*, c. 1662-63. Engraving, 49 × 58 cm. Amsterdam City Archive

INTERIOR OF THE OUDE KERK

1661

Emanuel de Witte
(Alkmaar 1617-1692 Amsterdam)

Panel, 101.5 × 121 cm
Signed and dated below, left: *E DeWitte Aº 1661*
Second signature, below right: *Je [...] 1734*
**On loan from Netherlands Institute for
Cultural Heritage**

Emanuel de Witte's painting shows the Oude Kerk from the southern transept looking north. The artist took a number of liberties with the actual architecture of the church. For example, he omitted the tie beams in the northern transept, and the giant candelabrum that hangs where the transepts cross the nave - which would have blocked the view of the organ. These omissions ensure a clear view of the window, and at the same time give a sense of space.

On the left in the nave, the pulpit is occupied by a preacher. Gathered round about him is a large group of worshippers. Behind the congregation, a smartly dressed gentleman accompanied by a dog, has stopped to listen. Three of the congregants have fallen asleep on the bench to the right.

On the far right, a family has just walked into view. De Witte emphasises these figures by casting sunlight on them. Since they appear to be meticulous, individual depictions, it seems probable that these figures are in fact portraits. Unfortunately we do not know who they were.

De Witte painted several pictures of this church. He also painted the northern transept from various vantage points, showing the organ which was renovated in 1657. Indeed, this may have been the occasion that prompted the Oude Kerk wardens to acquire the painting.

Emanuel de Witte was one of several Dutch artists who specialised in painting church interiors, even though biographers describe him as a difficult man who got on badly with his patrons. In his own day he was widely admired as an expert and master of perspective. In this painting, he used one-point perspective, placing the vanishing point along the right wall of the northern transept.

St Olof's was a medieval chapel alongside Sint Olofspoort. The chapel served as a temporary stock exchange from 1586 to 1602, when the building was once again dedicated to religious services as a Protestant church. Around 1645, St Olof's was rebuilt to form the chapel portrayed in the painting. It was renamed Oudezijds chapel, to match Nieuwezijds chapel, a church on the other side of the Amstel, on Kalverstraat.

Beerstraaten depicted the chapel's facade on Zeedijk in a snow-covered view of the city in winter. We are looking northwest, towards the harbour. Further along is the grindstone market. In 1618, Zeerecht was built there: the building in which the commissioners for maritime affairs met. Further along, the contours of Paalhuis on the New Bridge can be discerned. Like his contemporary Jan van der Heijden (see p. 73), Beerstraaten had no compunction about taking liberties with the street plan if it improved his composition. Here he depicts a far wider Zeedijk than it actually is at Oudezijds chapel. This enabled him to show the chapel from a less acute angle.

OUDEZIJDS OR ST OLOF'S CHAPEL
c. 1660-70

Abraham Beerstraaten
(Amsterdam 1643-after 1665)

Canvas, 89 × 105.3 cm
Signed, left on the wall beside the chapel entrance:
St. Olofs / Capel / A. Beerstraten / fecit /[date ?]
Loan Royal Antiquarian Society

It is morning on Dam Square. The Nieuwe Kerk sundial indicates nine o'clock. The sun is still low on the horizon as it shines on the recently completed Town Hall and the Nieuwe Kerk. Commerce has already started on the square. A man carrying a bundle on his back is walking towards the weigh house. A horse is drawing three barrels, possibly beer barrels. Further in the distance, four men, possibly merchants, are deep in conversation. The turban worn by the man on the left and the fez worn by the man on the right show Dam Square to have been a multicultural meeting place even then.

Van der Heyden had no qualms about adjusting the topography of the square to fit his composition. He moved the Nieuwe Kerk a long way to the right of its actual position. This gives an open view of the church, but at the expense of the new Town Hall and the weigh house, both of which are confined to the margins. This reveals the base for the uncompleted Nieuwe Kerk tower, which would in reality have been concealed behind the Town Hall.

Work had started on the tower in 1646, but construction stopped during the First Anglo-Dutch War (1652-54). The wooden roof which was later placed over the completed section can clearly be seen. While most of the structure was demolished in 1783, part remained and can still be seen today.

DAM SQUARE
c. 1668

Jan van der Heyden
(Gorinchem 1637-1712 Amsterdam)

Panel, 68 × 55 cm
Signed right, on the weigh house awning: *VHeyde*

This work, seen by some as the finest painting Dubbels ever made, depicts Marsdiep, the strait separating Texel from Den Helder. The island of Texel is left, the mainland is right. A large fleet of ships is passing through to the Zuiderzee (today's IJsselmeer). It was from Texel that Dutch merchantmen sailed; Dutch naval vessels sailed from Den Helder. There has been some speculation concerning the identity of this fleet. Many have suggested fleets departing for a battle, yet the ships in the painting are clearly returning to Dutch waters. Adriaan van der Hoop (1778-1854), the wealthy banker who bequeathed his superb collection of paintings to the city of Amsterdam, actually bought the work for its aesthetic quality. In his collection it was simply referred to as a marine view. Which fleet is shown and where the ships were heading was immaterial to him. In fact Dubbels used the same composition on several occasions, with different kinds of breakwater and different dune formations.

A FLEET AT DEN HELDER
c. 1667

Hendrick Dubbels
(Amsterdam 1621-1707 Amsterdam)

Canvas, 140 × 196 cm
Signed, below right on a piece of wood: *Dubbels*

We are looking from the north of a windswept IJ towards Amsterdam. On the other side we can easily make out the Oude Kerk, Town Hall on Dam Square and Nieuwe Kerk. But the real stars in this work are the magnificent vessels on the IJ. The two majestic pavilion barges with their decorated sterns left of centre, are the British barge *Mary*, a gift from Amsterdam to Charles II, and a Swedish craft, possibly the royal barge *Hjorten*.

The smaller barge to the right, striking sail, is flying a white flag with the arms of Prince Willem III (1650-1702). Until 1672, Amsterdam was anything but pro-Orange, so that the presence of the boat in the painting is rather surprising.

Further to the right is the barge of the States of Holland, with its gold flag and red lion emblem.

Perhaps the scene was intended as a political allegory. In 1668, Johan de Witt succeeded in forming a Triple Alliance with Sweden and Britain. The treaty was a response to the threat posed by the French. In the event, the alliance lasted barely two years. It was in that period that this painting appears to have been commissioned, possibly by an Amsterdammer with Orangist sympathies.

PARADE OF BARGES ON THE IJ
c. 1668-70

Ludolf Bakhuizen
(Emden 1630-1708 Amsterdam)

Canvas, 78 × 132 cm
Signed on the flag on the barge in the foreground:
Ludol. Backh.

In 1981, the museum bought a painting at a London art gallery entitled *Grocer Woman with Haarlemmerpoort in the Background* by Michiel van Musscher. A subsequent x-ray examination produced a surprising result: under the surface on the left was a carcass of a pig, stretched on a ladder, in the foreground on the left. Apparently, a former owner who objected to the display of pork had it painted over. In 1983, the overpainting was removed and the carcass was restored to view.

Stretched carcasses of pigs, oxen and cows were a popular theme in seventeenth-century art. Hanging the meat in this way allowed it to mature. Not before removing the organs however, since these would otherwise rot. That explains where the children found the pig's bladder

they are inflating. These two elements, the pig and the children playing with the bladder, may in fact be moral motifs referring to the transience of life.

Haarlemmerpoort was built between 1615 and 1618 by Hendrick de Keyser. It was demolished in 1837, to be replaced by the arch that currently stands on Haarlemmerplein.

A PIG ON A RACK WITH A VIEW OF HAARLEMMERPOORT 1668

Michiel van Musscher
(Rotterdam 1645-1705 Amsterdam)

Canvas, 87 × 75.5 cm
Dated on the side of the wheelbarrow: *1668*

This work shows the interior of a surgeon's workplace. An inscription on the reverse of the painting reveals the identity of the surgeon: Jacob Fransz Hercules (*c.* 1625-1708), who lived on Haarlemmerstraat. He was not an academically trained physician, more like an artisan who offered simple medical treatments. We see him here letting blood from his brother's arm, Thomas Hercules. The boy collecting the blood in a bowl is the surgeon's son, also Thomas. In the foreground, the woman of the house, Anna Jans ter Borgh, is sitting on a raised platform to protect against the cold. Beside her are the couple's other two children. The boy wearing a safety hat is their son Frans; the girl with the doll is Francijntje. An oval painting on the wall depicts Hercules, the family surname. On the wall above Anna Jans is a painting of an anatomy lesson. In the background an apprentice is shaving a customer. Two people are waiting their turn, while a man on crutches is entering the doorway.

This painting is hardly a snapshot of everyday activities at the surgeon's workplace; it is primarily a family portrait. Nevertheless, it provides a good impression of what a workplace would have looked like.

SURGEON JACOB FRANSZ HERCULES AND HIS FAMILY 1669

Egbert van Heemskerck
(Haarlem 1634-1704 London)

Canvas, 70 × 59 cm
Signed and dated, below right: *HKerck 1669*

Three family groups by Pieter de Hooch are known. This is the only one of these in which the subjects can be identified with certainty, thanks to the heraldic emblem, top left. These are members of the Jacott-Hoppesack family of Amsterdam

In the centre, in a striking silver satin dress is the woman of the house, Elisabeth Hoppesack (*c.* 1632/33-1670). Beside her, to the left, is her husband Jan Jacott (1632-after 1683), a cloth merchant. Their eldest son Balthasar (1658-1714) is standing behind his mother. He is motioning towards his sisters, Machtelina (1660-1701) and Elisabeth (1667-1672).

The interior in which the family is seated was probably an invention of De Hooch's. The palatial room, replete with marble, is reminiscent of the recently completed Town Hall on Dam Square (today's Royal Palace). The glimpse through the doorway into a garden leading to a classical building reflects the aristocratic idiom that came into fashion in the second half of the seventeenth century among Amsterdam's elite. It is certainly nothing like the house in which the family actually lived on Warmoesstraat.

THE JACOTT-HOPPESACK FAMILY
c. 1670

Pieter de Hooch
(Rotterdam 1629-1683/84 Amsterdam)

Canvas, 92.2 × 112.8 cm
Part of a monogram (?) right, at the entrance: P
Acquired with aid from the Rembrandt Society and the VSB Fonds

Cornelis Munter was the son of Joan Munter and Margaretha Geelvinck. His father, like Cornelis's grandfather Jan Cornelisz Geelvinck (see p. 46), served as a burgomaster of Amsterdam. Cornelis would eventually follow in their footsteps in 1706, although he soon found himself out of political office and died in 1708. Over twenty-five years earlier, when this portrait was painted, he was still at the outset of his career, as secretary of the city. Many details in the portrait refer to his profession. The folios and documents beside him on the pedestal, for example, and his place of work, the Town Hall on Dam Square, in the background. The relief of the barking dog on the pedestal is based on a design by Artus Quellinus that can still be

seen above the door of secretariat at the former Town Hall.

What really catches the eye is the green Japanese robe that Munster is wearing, which appears to have been painted with consummate ease and nonchalance. In fact Maes took great pains to create its smooth and shiny appearance. The elegant brushwork and the subject's relaxed pose combine to make this a vibrant portrait.

CORNELIS MUNTER
(1652-1708), 1679

Nicolaes Maes
(Dordrecht 1634-1693 Amsterdam)

Canvas, 56 × 47.5 cm
Signed and dated, left on the edge of the pedestal:
MAES. 1679

Berckheyde shows us Nieuwe-zijds Voorburgwal looking north, when it was still a canal. Further along is the recently completed Town Hall, with the dome that was put in place in 1665. While the building towers high above its neighbours, in this view of the city it merges effortlessly with its surroundings. On the square to the left, Bloemmarkt, a man is tethering his horse. Two well-dressed gentlemen are chatting in the shade of the trees along the canal. In the foreground, boatmen are rolling a barrel onto a barge. On the opposite side of the canal, people are walking to and from Dam Square. The beer boat and the horse-drawn cart on the bridge further in the distance connect the two sides in the composition.

Berckheyde, a native of Haarlem, specialised in painting views of cities. In Haarlem he painted numerous views of Grote Markt, the central square, from various angles and vantage points; so too in Amsterdam, where he portrayed new buildings such as the Town Hall and the recently finished bend in Heren-gracht (see p. 2-3 and opposite). There was clearly a large demand for paintings of these iconic locations.

BLOEMMARKT
c. 1670

Gerrit Berckheyde
(Haarlem 1638-1698 Haarlem)

Canvas, 45 × 61 cm
Signed on the boat: *gerrit Berck Heijde*

The bend in Herengracht where it meets Spiegelstraat was the most expensive section of the canal when the city undertook its fourth expansion in 1662. Berckheyde painted the new buildings on the bend several times; in most of these works some of the sites had yet to be built. This painting shows the completed construction, although not exactly as it was 1685. The house on the corner of Spiegelstraat, which catches the sun on the side (today it is Herengracht 464), was not completed until 1689. Topographical painters were quite willing to bend the truth for the sake of the composition: to show the viewer an unobstructed view of the magnificent classical facades, Berckheyde left out the newly planted trees along the canal.

The wealthy Amsterdammers who commissioned houses along this part of the canal generally bought two neighbouring plots of over seven metres wide, so that some of the facades are as wide as they are high.

THE BEND IN HERENGRACHT 1685

Gerrit Berckheyde
(Haarlem 1638-1698 Haarlem)

Canvas, 53 × 62 cm
Signed and dated, below left:
Gerret Berck Heyde 1685
On loan from the Rijksmuseum, Amsterdam

Kostverloren lay on a bend in the Amstel, between Amsterdam and Ouderkerk. At a time when most of the houses along the river were simple farmhouses this building, with its square tower and step gable, was an intriguing exception. The name Kostverloren means lost cost (the house was also called Ruysschenstein) and apparently refers to the huge sums needed to prop up the house as it sank in the marshy ground on the banks of the Amstel. Part of the building was demolished between 1659 and 1664.

Ruisdael shows the remains of the house in a forlorn state following the demolition. Only the tower stands amid the elms. The problem is obvious in the painting: as the land was drained, the water level fell, exposing and allowing the foundations to rot. Kostverloren was a popular theme among artists. The attraction of the ruin was due in part to its picturesque location on the Amstel. The building's sorry state drew many landscape artists. People would visit the ruins to enjoy the countryside round about.

MANOR KOSTVERLOREN ON THE AMSTEL
c. 1664

Jacob van Ruisdael
(Haarlem 1628/29-1682 Amsterdam)

Canvas, 63 × 75.5 cm
Monogrammed, below left: *JR*
Acquired with aid from the Rembrandt Society - Nationaal Fonds Kunstbehoud

Ruisdael painted this majestic panorama of Amsterdam around 1680. The city had grown considerably in the preceding years, with the completion of its concentric ring of canals.

Amsterdam is viewed here from the south, beneath one of Ruisdael's characteristically dramatic skies. The clouds cast a shadow over part of the city while other areas remain in the sun. In fact Ruisdael approached the city just as he approached his landscapes, as a stretch of land under the impact of nature.

The waters of the Amstel lead towards the bridge at Hoge Sluis, where today's Amstel Hotel stands.

Further back, the Zuiderkerk and Oude Kerk towers rise prominently. To the right of the bridge is one of the new embankments, with a mill at the corner. Further right, Weesperpoort was one of the entrances to the city. Even further right, is Oosterkerk, and glistening in the distant north lies the Buiten-IJ.

Left of centre stands the Town Hall on Dam Square, with the Westerkerk tower not far away. The gateway on the left is Utrechtse Poort, amid the mills that signal the course of Amsterdam's perimeter. Four industrial mills are depicted in the middle distance. These stood on Zaagmolensloot.

VIEW OF AMSTERDAM FROM AMSTELDIJK
c. 1680

Jacob van Ruisdael
(Haarlem 1628/29-1682 Amsterdam)

Canvas, 53.4 × 67.6 cm
Signed below left: JvRuisdael, with unclear date
Acquired with support from the Amsterdam
Municipality, Rembrandt Society, the
Jaffé-Pierson Stichting, the Mondriaan Stichting,
the VSB Fonds, the SNS Reaal Fonds, the Genootschap
Amsterdams Historisch Museum, the K.F. Hein Fonds
and various private benefactors.

Agnes Block (1629-1704), the woman in the centre of the painting, enjoyed a reputation in her own day as a botanist. She cultivated rare, exotic plants at Vijverhof, the estate shown here on the river Vecht near Loenen. The painting features some of her plants, including a Brazilian pineapple (far left) and a bulbous cactus from Curaçao. Part of her tropical greenhouse is visible on the extreme left. Block's curiosity was not confined to plants. As the prints, paintings, books and sculpture show, she had a wide interest in art and nature.

The man beside Agnes holding a small figurine is her second husband, Sybrand de Flines (1623-1697). She married this silk merchant of Amsterdam in 1674. They had no children. The identity of the two children on the left remains a mystery. De Flines had two daughters by his first marriage, but by 1694 they were in their thirties. Moreover, the child on the far left is more likely a boy than a girl. Nevertheless, it is probable that the children were in some way related to the couple.

AGNES BLOCK, SYBRAND DE FLINES AND TWO CHILDREN AT VIJVERHOF COUNTRY ESTATE
c. 1694

Jan Weenix
(Amsterdam c. 1640/41-1719 Amsterdam)

Canvas, 84 × 111 cm
Signed lower right: *J. Weenix fc*; traces of a date
Acquired with aid from the Rembrandt Society

For painters in the flourishing art market of the seventeenth century it was generally necessary to specialise in a genre. This was often the only way to stave off rivals. Melchior d'Hondecoeter made himself master of an exquisite genre. He specialised in birds. In fact Houbraken, the famous biographer of Dutch artists, made the slightly incredible claim that Hondecoeter kept a rooster as a model which he 'placed beside his easel, and using his mahlstick he would tilt the head up or down, turn the body left or right, with wings stretched or as if walking, and which would then remain motionless in that position' until Hondecoeter had finished painting.

In this painting the foreground is full of birds of various species. Yet the building in the background is equally remarkable: the new Town Hall on Dam Square, which the poet Vondel (see p. 56) celebrated as the eighth wonder of the world. The building was a popular feature in paintings by Amsterdam artists of the second half of the seventeenth century (see p. 2-3 and 80). Apart from city views, the Town Hall appears in many portraits, and Hondecoeter followed the fashion in his own unique way.

BIRDS ON A BALUSTRADE WITH THE TOWN HALL IN THE BACKGROUND 1670

Melchior d'Hondecoeter
(Utrecht 1636-1695 Amsterdam)

Canvas, 183.5 × 162 cm
Signed and dated, below right on the edge of the balustrade: *M D'hondecoeter ft. 1670*

The Bourse, built in 1608-13 after a design by Hendrick de Keyser, stood on Rokin, just south of Dam Square. In 1668-70, the Bourse was extended after a design by Daniel Stalpaert. It was shortly after this that Job Berckheyde painted the new section of the stock exchange courtyard. Part of the statue of Mercury that adorned the classical facade can be seen through the arcade window.

Groups of traders are milling about the courtyard, especially under the arcade. Notices on the columns state where the traders are based and where they trade. The two oriental gentlemen, with their colourful coats and hats, reflect Amsterdam's position as a centre of international commerce.

To judge from the shadows, the painting seems to show the Bourse at around midday: the exchange has just opened. Business hours were between twelve and two in the afternoon. In fact the regulations had to be tightened, since traders would often use Dam Square to do business before and after the exchange opened. Many preferred to run the risk of a fine rather than lose out on a deal.

COURTYARD OF HENDRICK DE KEYSER'S BOURSE
c. 1680

Job Berckheyde
(Haarlem 1630-1693 Haarlem)

Canvas, 89 × 116 cm
Signed on the base of the column, right: *Job Berckheyde*

De Lairesse painted this allegory around 1680, probably as a design for one of the lunettes in the burgher hall at the Town Hall on Dam Square. However, the work was never realised. De Lairesse lost his sight in 1689.

In the centre of the painting, the personification of Amsterdam is seated on a throne; flanked by the emblem and a map of the city. Behind her are personifications of (left to right) Charity, Faith, Unity and Justice. Floating above her is Fame, sounding two trumpets. Left, holding a rudder and wearing a crown of ships, is the river god of the IJ; right, opposite him, is the river god of the Amstel. Beside him is a woman with the attributes of Mercury, embracing a cornucopia, or horn of plenty.

The significance of the depiction, as with Berchem's allegory of *c.* 1663 (see p. 69), is that Amsterdam owes its wealth to its maritime commerce, while the virtues and positive attributes gathered behind the personification of Amsterdam ensure that the city's trade succeeds.

ALLEGORY OF THE FAME OF AMSTERDAM
c. 1680

Gerard de Lairesse
(Liège 1641-1711 Amsterdam)

Canvas, 46.5 × 62 cm
Monogrammed, below right: *G.L.*

The lecturer giving this anatomy lesson is the man holding the scalpel, Frederik Ruysch (1638-1731), one of the most renowned physicians of the early modern period. In 1665, at the age of 27, Ruysch had discovered the valves of the lymphatic vessels which ensure that the lymph flows in the right direction. In this group portrait he is demonstrating the lymph vessels of the groin. In practice, an anatomy lesson would never begin with this area. Corpses were not preserved before being dissected, so a prudent anatomist would start with the parts of the body that decay first.

The portrait appears to emphasise the scientific character of anatomy. Perhaps that is why Backer decorated the room with statues of Galen (130-201) and the god of medicine, Asklepios. He places the lecture in a context of scholarship stretching back to classical antiquity.

It is interesting that the scientific study of human anatomy, which began in the Renaissance, brought an end to a period in medical history of more than a thousand years in which the principal foundation for medical practice had been the ideas of Galen. Ruysch was portrayed again in 1683, by Jan van Neck (see opposite).

THE ANATOMY LESSON OF DR FREDERIK RUYSCH 1670

Adriaen Backer
(Amsterdam 1630-1684 Amsterdam)

Canvas, 168 × 244 cm
Remains of signature and date,
below centre: *... f 1670*

This painting is the second anatomy lesson featuring the famous physician Frederik Ruysch. Here Ruysch is dissecting a stillborn child to show how the blood flows through the placenta. Ruysch enjoyed an international reputation for his dissections and preservation of specimens. He demonstrates his skills as a dissector in this painting. Ruysch's fame was such that he sold most of his anatomical collection to Peter the Great when the tsar visited Holland in 1697-98 (see p. 93).

That Van Neck featured an infant as the subject of an anatomy lesson is exceptional. Perhaps it was connected to the anatomist's position as the city's supervisor of midwives. It seems unlikely that this lecture actually took place in the dissecting theatre maintained by the Surgeons' Guild above the Kleine Vleeshal meat market on Nes from 1639 to 1691.

The boy on the right is the lecturer's son, Hendrick Ruysch (1673-1727). Together with his sister, the celebrated painter Rachel Ruysch (1664-1750), he helped the anatomist assemble his famous collection of specimens.

THE ANATOMY LESSON OF DR FREDERIK RUYSCH 1683

Jan van Neck
(Naarden 1634/35-1714 Amsterdam)

Canvas, 142 × 203 cm
Signed and dated, below right on the skeleton stand:
J V Neck / Contrarolleur / f. 1683

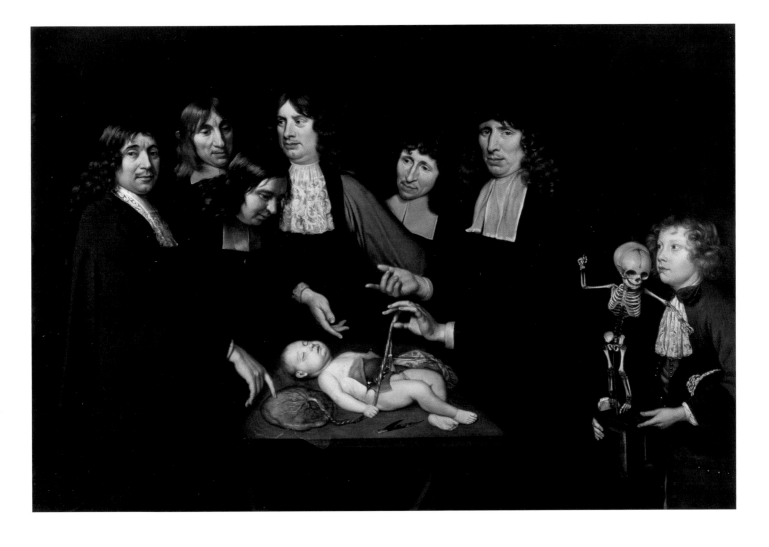

89

THE GOUDEN LEEUW ON THE IJ AT AMSTERDAM
1686

Willem van de Velde
(Leiden 1633-1704 London)

Canvas, 179.5 × 316 cm
Signed and dated on a piece of driftwood, left of centre:
W.v. Velde J. 1686

This monumental painting shows Amsterdam from the opposite bank of the IJ, a position from which many artists have portrayed the city. Here the focus is not the city, however, but the harbour. To the right are the Zuiderkerk and Schreierstoren. Left of these, the harbour stretches out to the islands east of the city, with the tower of the East Indies maritime depot rising above the buildings of Amsterdam's shipyard (see p. 92).

It was here that the huge battleship that dominates this painting was launched in 1666: the *Gouden Leeuw*. This was the flagship of Amsterdam's Admirality, the ship that achieved such fame in the Third Anglo-Dutch War (1672-74) under command of Cornelis Tromp (1629-1691). Van de Velde painted the moment when, after twenty years of loyal service, the *Gouden Leeuw* returned on its final voyage to Amsterdam harbour for demolition.

The ship is welcomed with all due honours. In the foreground, a barge is sailing up the IJ to greet the *Gouden Leeuw*. To the left, a state barge is firing a salute. Numerous other small boats have gathered to see the famous warship and show their respect.

Van de Velde was probably commissioned to paint the work by the harbourmasters of Amsterdam: the Oppercommissarissen der Walen. *Walen* (sing. *waal*) were the pools on either side of the city where most of the harbour activity took place. A view of Amsterdam's harbour would have been a logical choice for the harbourmasters. The *Gouden Leeuw* gives the setting a historical dimension: the harbour where famous large ships are built.

The office of the harbourmasters was at Schreierstoren. It is clear from the painting that Van de Velde had originally painted a larger version of this building, doubtlessly to emphasise his patrons' headquarters. In the end, he reduced it, conforming to its actual dimensions. The painting was displayed in the harbourmasters' boardroom, where it remained until 1808. The huge canvas must have looked impressive in the confined space of Schreierstoren.

The shipyard of the Dutch East India Company (Verenigde Oostindische Compagnie or VOC) lay east of the harbour, on the island of Oostenburg. Many of the ships that sailed to the Far East were built here. A new vessel under construction is shown in the foreground. Behind it, firing a salute, is the barge of Amsterdam's VOC chamber. A ship is careened to the right - weighed down to one side by its mast to enable repair and maintenance of the hull. Shipyard workers are busy scorching the bottom clean. Back at the yard itself, work on another ship has just started, while to the far left lies a finished eastindiaman in all its glory. The vessel is called 't Wapen van Oost-Indien, an appropriate name, yet entirely the artist's own invention. No such ship ever sailed.

The building in the background is the VOC maritime depot or Oost-Indisch Zeemagazijn: a building 180 metres long, symbolic of the company's power. Ropewalks can be seen to the far left. At that time, the VOC depot and shipyard formed the largest industrial complex in the world. In 1822, less than twenty-five years after the company's liquidation, the depot collapsed, having been allowed to decay.

THE SHIPYARD OF THE DUTCH EAST INDIA COMPANY
1696

Ludolf Bakhuizen
(Emden 1630-1708 Amsterdam)

Canvas, 126 × 142 cm
Signed below right on the anchor: L. BAKHUIZ;
dated below left, on the mooring post: *1696*
On loan from Netherlands Institute for Cultural Heritage

To celebrate the visit of the Muscovite Tsar Peter the Great in 1697, a mock battle was staged on the IJ. The tsar is the figure in red on the barge to the left, flying the white-blue-and-red Muscovite pennant.

Mock battles were spectacular events in which two squadrons of warships pretended to fight. Casper Luyken (1672-1708) described the show recorded in this painting. 'The houses in the surrounding Waterland villages shook with the noise of the incessant gunfire, since the volunteers loosed continual salvos whenever the barge carrying the embassy passed by. The whole Y was full of all kinds of vessels as far as the eye could see, gathered there to witness this rare event.'

The painting shows the first phase of the battle: the fighting between individual ships. Although this was not a real battle, the damage was nevertheless considerable. That was not due to gunfire, but to the tendency of parched captains to quench their thirst with something a little more refreshing. Because of the damage, the following Admiralty parade had to be cancelled.

Peter the Great had come to Holland to study the shipbuilding industry. He had visited the shipyards of Zaandam the previous week and had worked there on a frigate being built at a VOC yard (see opposite) and consequently named after him: the *Pieter en Paul*.

MOCK BATTLE ON THE IJ IN HONOUR OF THE EMBASSY FROM MOSCOW
c. 1697-1700

Abraham Storck
(Amsterdam 1644-1708 Amsterdam)

Canvas, 50 × 66 cm
Signed, below left on a boat: *A: Storck: Fecit*

Whaling could be a lucrative enterprise. The blubber was refined to make train for products such as lamp oil, candles and soap. This painting combines different aspects of the fishery. The larger ship on the left is leading the chase. This is the *Admirael Willem Bastiaensz* commanded by Dirk Slang. To the right *De Jager*, commanded by Jacob Jansz Rijkers, is hoisting slabs of whale on board. Rijkers, whose initials I. R. appear on the stern of the longboats, sailed under commission of the Amsterdam shipowner Gerrit Doornekroon. In the distance, between the two ships, is a third whaler, *De Faam*.

In the foreground, men on the ice are dragging a dead whale out of the water; further along, a man is tackling a polar bear with a stick. The ship on the right, enclosed by the ice, reminds the viewer that whaling could be perilous. In 1703, no less than 23 whalers failed to return.

Dutch whalers originally hunted in the seas west of Norway. In the 1670s, their focus gradually shifted further north and west as the whale populations collapsed. Later, they sailed as far as Davis Strait, west of Greenland.

GERRIT DOORNEKROON'S WHALING FLEET
c. 1703

Adriaen van Salm
(Delfshaven 1660-1720 Delfshaven)

Panel, 108 × 177 cm
Signed below right: *A. Salm Fecit*

In 1706, Jonas Witsen (1667-1715) signed an unusual contract with Dirk Valkenburg. He undertook to go to Suriname and to work there for four years as Witsen's bookkeeper and as a painter, with permission to travel around 'to paint views of all three plantations as well as other rare birds and plants.' Recent research has revealed that this painting shows Witsen's Waterlant plantation, which lay on the east bank of the Suriname river.

Valkenburg depicted the plantation from the opposite bank, based on sketches he had made earlier. The large building in the centre is the sugar mill and the refinery where the sugar was boiled.

Behind this are the distillery and the slave house. The building on the right, the only brick-built structure, is the home of the plantation manager. On the far left is a sluice.

Among the boats on the river is a barge with which the planter would have visited Paramaribo and other plantations. It was rowed by slaves: the more slaves rowing the barge, the higher the planter's status. This barge belonged to the plantation manager.

Valkenburg did not complete his four-year contract. The Surinamese climate began to affect his health and after two years he returned to Amsterdam.

WATERLANT SUGAR PLANTATION IN SURINAME
c. 1708

Dirk Valkenburg
(Amsterdam 1675-1721 Amsterdam)

Canvas, 31.5 × 47.5
Monogrammed below left: *D. VB* [V and B combined]

Troost presents a scene from a farce by Jacob Alewijn: *Beslikte Swaentje en drooge Fobert of de Boere rechtbank* (Swelling Swaentje and Sullen Fobert, or the Village Court). Both Troost and his wife, Maria van Duijn (b. 1695), acted in plays at Amsterdam's Schouwburg theatre. It is no surprise, therefore, that Troost often drew from the theatre for subjects. This scene from *Beslikte Swaentje* is the earliest known painting by Troost with a theatrical setting.

The farce tells the story of Swaentje, a young, beautiful yet rather frivolous village woman. In the painting she is identified by her red dress, embroidered with a swan.

She has fallen for the charms of the Jonker Jan, standing beside her. Jan is the son of the lord of Puyterveen, the fictional village in which the story is set. The dim-witted Fobert Melis, in tears on the left, has been blamed for Swaentje's predicament, so her parents have demanded that he marry her. Crelis Melis, Fobert's father standing beside the unfortunate lad, has refused to accept this and so the case has come to court. The play and the painting make a mockery of the two lawyers and the justice meted out at Puyterveen. The trial ends by concluding that Fobert and Swaentje must marry.

THE VILLAGE COURT IN 'BESLIKTE SWAANTJE', A FARCE

1727

Cornelis Troost
(Amsterdam 1696-1750 Amsterdam)

Panel, triptych, total 111 × 129 cm
Signed and dated, top left: C. Troost.f.1727

Jan van Huysum was known for the virtuosity of his floral still lifes. In fact his bouquets were generally imaginary: they combined flowers that could never have bloomed at the same time. This work is certainly no exception.

A female figure features on the vase. This may be Flora, the goddess of flowers. A Dutch inscription either side of her is taken from Christ's Sermon on the Mount (Matthew 6:28-29). Much of the text is hidden behind leaves and tendrils. The complete verses are as follows: 'So why do you worry about clothing? Consider the lilies of the field, how they grow: they neither toil nor spin; and yet I say to you that even Solomon in all his glory was not arrayed like one of these.' Christ's message is that we should not attach value to worldly matters,

for nature needs no embellishment. The verse gives this apparently purely decorous vase of flowers an additional moral content. Yet the rather clumsy way the inscription is written - taking no account of the curve of the vase - suggests that the biblical quotation was inserted at a later date by someone other than Van Huysum.

STILL LIFE WITH FLOWERS, 'LILIES OF THE FIELDS'

c. 1720-30

Jan van Huysum
(Amsterdam 1682-1749 Amsterdam)

Canvas, 66.5 × 52 cm
Signed below right on the plinth: *JanVanHuysumfecit*

When Abraham Titsingh (1684-1776), the surgeon on the right of the painting, was appointed to the board of the Surgeons' Guild in 1731, he found the organisation riddled by fraud, including the sale of forged surgeon's certificates and embezzlement of money from the widows' fund. Titsingh refused to accept the proffered bribes and brought the case to the attention of the burgomasters, who replaced the entire board. The new board decided shortly after their appointment in 1732 to commission 'a painting, each paying from their own pocket without charge to the guild, and to donate the painting to the guild, in which the governors as named shall be portrayed by the honourable Mr Quinkhard, painter, in memory of their appointment to reform the guild.'

Quinkhard included some obvious references to the reform of the guild. The portrait on the wall of lecturer Willem Röell (1700-1775) is inscribed *Vigilate Juste* (Vigilance and Justice). The surgeon's certificate held by Bartholomeus Vermeij, the governor on the left, is a clear rebuke to the deposed governors. The portrait was presented and displayed in the guild room on 15 September 1732. Each of the governors paid Quinkhard 100 guilders.

THE GOVERNORS OF THE SURGEONS' GUILD
1732

Jan Maurits Quinkhard
(Rees 1688-1772 Amsterdam)

Canvas, 176.5 × 273 cm
Signed and dated on the inkstand:
J.M. Quinckhard pinxit 1732

ALLEGORY OF THE WRITING OF HISTORY

1754

Jacob de Wit
(Amsterdam 1695-1754 Amsterdam)

Canvas, 295 × 105 cm
Signed and dated on a dossier, right:
J de Wit [**joined**] / *F.* / *1754*

De Wit was the leading painter of ceilings and other interior decorations in Amsterdam in the early eighteenth century. This allegory was painted for the library at the home of Isaac de Pinto (1717-1787) on Nieuwe Herengracht (today, number 99). It was positioned between two doors leading to the garden. The painting's original location is reflected in the medallion at the bottom of the work. As the surrounding inscription states, it shows Ptolemy II Philadelphus (*c*. 309-247 BC), the Egyptian king who established the famous library at Alexandria. The three cherubs, busy with their books and manuscripts, also refer to the room's function as a library.

The top half of the painting epitomises the ultimate purpose of the knowledge of books and learning: this is a personification of the writing of history. The female nude at the summit is Truth. Naked, because she has nothing to hide, yet covered with a cloth, since no one can ever know her completely. To the left, wearing a helmet, is Pallas Athena, the Greek goddess who epitomises Wisdom here. She and the naked truth together instruct Clio, the muse of history, as she writes.

Jan de Bosch (1713-1785) is central to this portrait. It is he who seems to be introducing the rest of the family with a gesture of the hand. With his other hand he is holding a portrait of his late mother, Judith Willink (1679-1747). Jan, a Mennonite, worked as a bookkeeper at the Amsterdam exchange bank. On the left, his brother Jeronimo de Bosch II is standing behind his wife Catharina van der Heyden. Seated beside her, further left, are the eldest brother Bernardus and his wife Margaretha van Leuvenig. And on the far left, the *pater familias* Jeronimo de Bosch I (1677-1767). Seated on our side of the table is Jan's sister, Elizabeth, beside her husband Willem Schuyt, a Mennonite preacher. The young man who just walked in on the right is the youngest brother, Hendrik.

The family presented itself here as art-loving burghers. On the table lies a folio; beside it a drawing or print. Bernardus de Bosch and his wife are admiring another print. The cupboard against the back wall is typical of the cabinets in which burghers kept their collections of art and other curiosities. The figure depicted on the door is Pictura, a personification of art. The cabinet door, a painting by Jacob de Wit (1695-1754), has survived. It can be seen at the Amsterdam Historical Museum, on loan from the Rijksmuseum.

JAN DE BOSCH AND HIS FAMILY
1754

Tibout Regters
(Dordrecht 1710-1768 Amsterdam)

Canvas, 77 × 98 cm
Signed and dated,
left on the plinth: *T. Regters / Pinxit 1754*

When the museum purchased this group portrait by Hendrik Pothoven at auction in 1964, it was undoubtedly hoped that researchers would soon succeed in identifying the figures seated around the table. Unfortunately, their names are still a mystery.

Grouped about a table in a comfortable room are two men, a woman and two children. Visible through the window is a courtyard, backing on to a summer house with a bust on a ledge.

The relationship of the figures to one another can only be guessed at. The portrait in the centre is presumably of a woman who had recently died, perhaps the wife of the older man on the left. It seems logical to assume that one of the younger adults is a child of this man. Based on the order in which they are arranged, it seems reasonable to conclude that the woman is the daughter, and the man behind her, her husband, while the two children are their offspring.

The key to an identification may lie in the summer house that can be seen through the window. The spire in the background belongs to the Begijnhof's English church. From that geographical clue it may be possible to locate the address of the house in which these people are posing for their portrait, and to find out who lived there at the time.

FAMILY IN AN INTERIOR
1774

Hendrik Pothoven
(Amsterdam 1725-1807 The Hague)

Canvas, 66.5 × 52 cm
Signed and dated, below left on the plinth:
H.Pothoven A° 1774

MINT TOWER SEEN FROM SINGEL CANAL

1751

Jan ten Compe
(Amsterdam 1713-1761 Amsterdam)

Panel, 56 × 75.5 cm
Signed and dated on the boat on the left bank of the canal:
J.T.Compe f 1751

The Mint, originally built around 1480, began life as the western tower of Regulierspoort. All but the base of a tower and the adjacent guardhouse was destroyed in a fire in 1619. A year later, a new tower was added to the base, designed by Hendrick de Keyser. When the mint at Dordrecht stopped producing coinage in 1672 – a catastrophic year in Dutch history – the former town gate was given a new use. It was then that it received its present name. When Ten Compe painted the Mint, the building was a boardinghouse. In 1884, the former guardhouse was demolished to make way for the current structure.

Jan ten Compe, who had been raised at Amsterdam's Diaconal orphanage, was one of the leading specialists in city views in the eighteenth century. He clearly drew inspiration from seventeenth-century predecessors such as Jan van der Heyden and Gerrit Berckheyde, yet also added new elements and themes in his many views of Amsterdam.

In this depiction of Singel canal where it meets the Mint, a subject that Berckheyde and Van der Heyden never painted, the tower dominates the scene against a moderately cloudy sky. To the left, we see through to Schapenmarkt (today's Muntplein) and in the distance the Zuiderkerk tower. On the right, Ten Compe increased the sense of depth by showing the area beyond the bridge and the houses along Binnen-Amstel. The many people and animals on the canalside and the bridge are extras; the main characters are the city's buildings in the midday sun.

Below, to the right, a beer barrel is floating on the water. It is marked with a swan. Perhaps it belonged to De Zwaan brewery, which stood further along on Singel. In Ten Compe's depiction of the barrel, the swan seems to be swimming on the water. Presumably this was a subtle visual joke rather than a topographical reference to the nearby brewery.

The work was purchased from the artist himself by the collector Gerret Braamcamp for 400 guilders in 1752. On 31 July 1777, six years after Braamcamp's death, his collection was put up for auction. In 1936, after travelling back and forth, the work finally returned to Amsterdam.

Jan de Beijer earned his living drawing topographical views. He worked for leading print publishers and collectors, such as Isaac Tirion, Cornelis Ploos van Amstel and Pierre Fouquet. Paintings by De Beijer are rare. This work is a remarkably convincing example from this limited oeuvre.

De Beijer probably painted the scene from a jetty on the IJ where it meets Singel canal. This is the site of the western end of the artificial island on which today's Central Station stands: Stationseiland.

The characteristic tower is Haringpakkerstoren. The building underneath was where the herring shipped to the city was packed. It was also home to several guilds, while its upper storeys were used as a watchtower by the harbour authorities. The golden herring at the top of Hendrick de Keyser's tower is clearly visible, providing an appropriate finial. In 1829, the tower was demolished. In the distance, rising above the houses, is the dome of the nearby Lutheren church.

The sluice in the foreground is Nieuwe Haarlemmersluis, with a bridge linking Nieuwendijk and Haarlemmerstraat. Further right is a bridge crossing Brouwersgracht.

HARINGPAKKERSTOREN VIEWED FROM THE IJ
c. 1765-70

Jan de Beijer
(Aarau 1703-1780 Kleve)

Panel, 45,5 × 61 cm
Signed on the boat, left: *De Beyer*

De Lelie was much in demand as a portrait painter around 1800 (see p. 106-107). He was also a prolific painter of so-called genre pieces, paintings of scenes from everyday life. For his themes and style he drew on the work of seventeenth-century masters of genre painting, such as Vermeer, Pieter de Hooch and Nicolaas Maes. Many have commented on the similarity between this painting and Vermeer's famous *Milkmaid*, which was in Jan Jacob de Bruijn's collection in Amsterdam in 1796. Perhaps De Lelie saw it there. It was widely admired by artists and connoisseurs of the day. As in Vermeer's work, a kitchen maid is busy doing her chores, against a plain wall with a kitchen utensil suspended on a nail.

Unlike Vermeer's *Milkmaid*, this young woman is lit from the right. Another difference is the concentration with which Vermeer's maid pours the milk. De Lelie's maid is distracted, perhaps by someone entering the kitchen. By showing her looking towards us, De Lelie gives us the sense that we are the visitor entering the kitchen. This trick was often employed by seventeenth-century artists.

WOMAN SCOURING A PAN
1796

Adriaan de Lelie
(Tilburg 1755-1820 Amsterdam)

Panel 25.4 × 21.8 cm
Signed and dated, above left: *..elie ft. 1796*

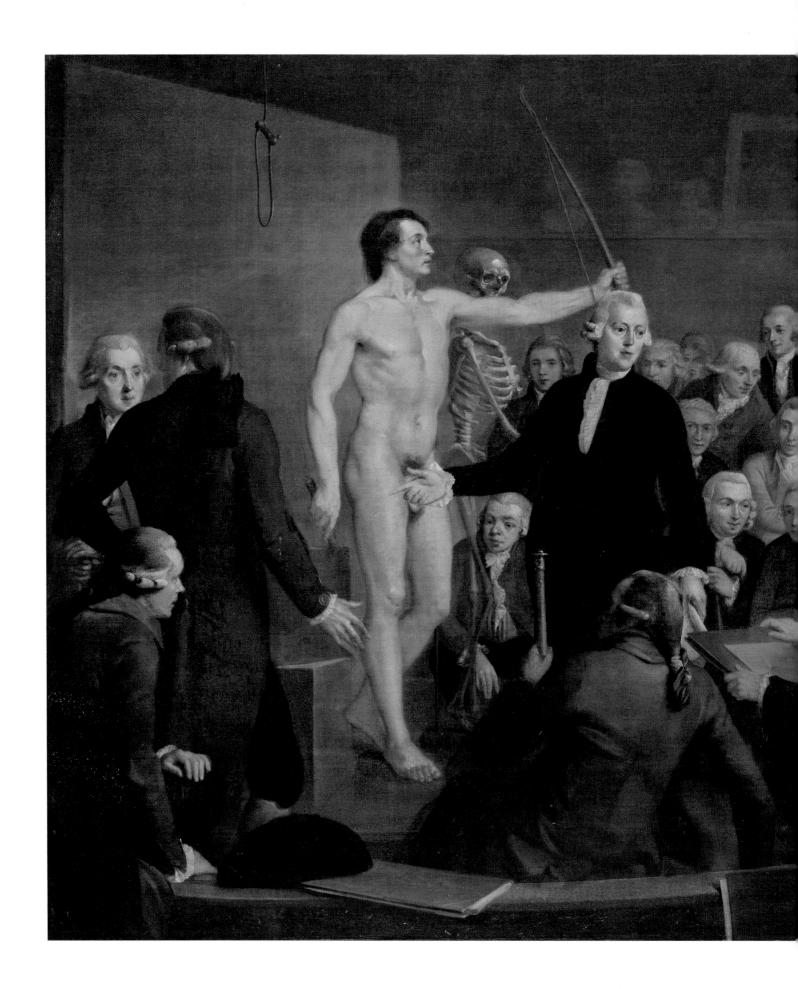

ANATOMY LECTURE BY ANDREAS BONN AT THE DEPARTMENT OF DRAWING OF FELIX MERITIS

1792

Adriaan de Lelie
(Tilburg 1755-1820 Amsterdam)

Canvas, 81 × 100 cm
Signed and dated, right of centre on the folder against the balustrade:
A. de Lelie fec. 1792

Adriaen de Lelie joined Felix Meritis on 24 September 1787. New members of the society were charged an entrance fee. At the drawing department the practice was to submit this in kind, generally in the form of a work of art. De Lelie fulfilled his obligation on 1 December 1792 with 'a very nice and deserving painting depicting a demonstration of the muscles on a nude model by Professor A. Bonn, anatomist and surgeon, in the art studio of our department, incorporating the aforementioned Professor Bonn and all the audience of members portrayed from life'.

The minutes of the drawing department record various lectures of this nature, although it is quite possible that the lecture by Professor Bonn on muscular anatomy may not actually have taken place as depicted here.

The art studio was on the third floor of the society's building on Keizersgracht, which opened there in 1788. The room had been specially built to enable artists to draw to an academic standard. The architects had taken account of the need for sufficient light, and a stage was provided for the models to stand on. The model shown here is in fact standing on the stage. Behind the canvas is a stove, to stop him catching cold. The model is standing in the pose of the famous statue of Apollo Belvedere, now at the Vatican.

With this De Lelie adds an extra academic element to the lecture. Apollo Belvedere was the ultimate example of anatomical perfection in the academic tradition. De Lelie showed the model in this pose to place the lecture on muscular anatomy in an artistic context. This element enabled him to encapsulate two aspects of academic draughtsmanship as practised at Felix Meritis in a single subject, combining drawing from (classical) sculpture and drawing from life.

In a description of Felix Meritis written in 1800, Cornelis Sebille Roos (1754-1820) discusses the painting. He recalls how, in the boardroom of the drawing department he saw numerous works of art, including 'an extremely fine painting showing the art studio in which the members of the departments are listening attentively to a lecture on muscular anatomy by Professor A. Bonn illustrated by a nude model, and in which all the portraits of the persons present are painted with excellent accuracy'.

General

E.R. Mandle and J.W. Niemeijer, *Dutch Masterpieces from the 18th Century: Paintings and Drawings 1700-1800* (exhibition catalogue), Minneapolis / Toledo / Philadelphia 1971.

Bob Haak, *The Golden Age: Dutch Painters of the Seventeenth Century,* New York 1984.

Svetlana Alpers, *The Art of Describing: Dutch Art in the Seventeenth Century*, London 1983.

Willy Halsema-Kubes, Reinier Baarssen and Wouter Kloek (eds), *Art before the Iconoclasm: Northern Netherlandish art 1525-1580,* Amsterdam / The Hague 1986.

Ger Luijten and Wouter Kloek (eds.), *Dawn of the Golden Age: Northern Netherlandish Art 1580-1620* (exhibition catalogue), Amsterdam / Zwolle 1993.

Mariet Westermann, *The Art of the Dutch Republic 1585-1718 / A Worldly Art: The Dutch Republic, 1585-1718*, New York 1996.

Seymour Slive, *Dutch Painting, 1600-1800,* New Haven 1995.

Norbert Middelkoop *et al.*, *De Oude Meesters van de stad Amsterdam* (collection catalogue), Amsterdam 2008.

Genres

Peter Sutton (ed.), *Masters of Seventeenth-Century Dutch Genre Painting* (exhibition catalogue), Philadelphia / Berlin / London 1984.

Peter Sutton (ed.), *Masters of 17th-Century Dutch landscape painting* (exhibition catalogue), Boston 1987.

George Keyes (ed.) *Mirror of Empire: Dutch Marine Art of the Seventeenth Century* (exhibition catalogue), Minneapolis 1990.

Wayne Franits, *Looking at Seventeenth-Century Dutch Art: Realism Reconsidered*, Cambridge 1997.

Jeroen Giltaij and Jan Kelch (eds), *Praise of ships and the sea: The Dutch marine painters of the 17th century*, Rotterdam / Berlin 1996.

Alois Riegl, *The Group Portraiture of Holland,* Los Angeles 1999.

Alan Chong and Wouter Kloek (eds), *Still-Life Paintings from the Netherlands 1550-1720*, Amsterdam / Cleveland 1999.

Mariet Westermann (ed.), *Art & Home: Dutch Interiors in the Age of Rembrandt* (exhibition catalogue), Denver / Newark 2001.

Norbert Middelkoop (ed.), Kopstukken: *Portretten van Amsterdammers 1600-1800* (exhibition catalogue), Amsterdam 2002.

Wayne Franits, *Dutch Seventeenth-Century Genre Painting: Its Stylistic and Thematic Evolution*, New Haven 2004.

Rudi Ekkart, Quentin Buvelot and Marieke de Winkel (eds), *Dutch Portraits: The Age of Rembrandt and Frans Hals* (exhibition catalogue), The Hague / London 2007.

Ariane van Suchtelen and Arhur Wheelock (eds), *Dutch Cityscapes of the Golden Age* (exhibition catalogue), The Hague / Washington 2008.

For an extensive list of books about Dutch and Flemish art, visit www.codart.nl/curators-bookshelf

History

Jonathan Israel, *The Dutch Republic: Its Rise, Greatness and Fall 1477-1806*, Oxford 1995.

Simon Schama, *The Embarrassment of Riches: An Interpretation of Dutch Culture in the Golden Age*, New York 1987.